I Think I Took A Wrong Turning Somewhere!

A Book of Poems and Thoughts

by
David Cope

Bloomington, IN Milton Keynes, UK
authorHOUSE®

AuthorHouse™
1663 Liberty Drive, Suite 200
Bloomington, IN 47403
www.authorhouse.com
Phone: 1-800-839-8640

AuthorHouse™ UK Ltd.
500 Avebury Boulevard
Central Milton Keynes, MK9 2BE
www.authorhouse.co.uk
Phone: 08001974150

First published by AuthorHouse 7/5/2007

ISBN: 978-1-4259-9720-5 (sc)

Printed in the United States of America
Bloomington, Indiana

This book is printed on acid-free paper.

Dedications,:

There are a number of people who I want to dedicate this book to:

Firstly, my mother. My mum believed in me and she also loved poetry. She never had the opportunity to explore her talents but loved verse in its many forms.

Next there is my mum in law Mary, who has been a constant source of inspiration and support, and also someone who has stood strong in her convictions giving me a reason to continue.

Revd Jane Atkins is featured in this book and is as instrumental as any living person in bringing me to faith, but also recognising the talent and encouraging that talent in the name of the Lord, despite my own self...

My good friends in all the Churches all over the place!

Bhupinder and Harbinder, for their support and belief when times looked impossible,

And last but not least, Genesta for putting up with me for all these years.

Contents

List of Poems

Chapter One
"Here We Go Again"

Here I am sitting at a blank screen on the PC and trying to find the right words to compliment a second book of poems. This second book contains a number of poems that I have written and that have been on my mind since I suppose, I put the last book together which right now seems like an eternity ago. That book to date is unpublished but if any reader feels compelled to read it, I'm sure that I can prevail upon the publishers to have a look at it.

It seems to me that an awful lot has happened to me and the world since that first little book was written back in 2000. There has been September the 11th attack where the Americans and many others suffered at the hands of the misguided at best, and terrorists at worst. I cannot begin to express my thoughts that associate with those awful events, but let's face it, the world is always providing a challenge where the lives of human beings are concerned. Then there has been quite recently, the conflict in Iraq which has been much debated and many view points raised. But the conflict in the world seems never ending, Kosova, Ruwanda, Israel, the list goes on. And on top of all of this there's been the natural disasters which also defy comprehension, so what is the point of writing the poems that I do and indeed the ones in this book? Well maybe they strike home somewhere and with someone, maybe you!

I believe that where Christians are concerned and some of us on the edge of that perspective, are moved by something, and that 'something' is the body of Christ moving in the world and using us as we are all part of that (we believe), so I leave the judgement on that to you who have taken the time to read this book. I also hope that you're not put off by that before exploring what I've tried to put into the book, and more especially the poems themselves.

The last book I wrote was a bit of an experiment really, contained a lot of poems that had come about as a result of the death of my Mum (Often a method of grieving or healing when faced with that sort of trauma), the year I spent as Mayor in Hinckley and Bosworth and a sort of finding me whatever that means.

During my time as Mayor both my wife Genesta and I spent a lot of time in civic services in many Churches all over Leicestershire and significantly we had, nationally, the first Holocaust remembrance services, another momentous issue that beset the world all those years ago, but still as relevant today as ever it was, given the events throughout the world in recent times.

Well since I last put words together as a book, I have also had some time of reflection, and some lessons in Christianity that have made me consider the way of Christian faith more carefully, for the way is littered with the lost hopes and aspirations of the Christian who thought that they had got it right and in fact had not. We are all learning all the time and the person who tells you that they have the complete grasp of it, is not only deluding you but themselves as well in my humble opinion.

So the book that you have before you has again come from the inner recesses of me, and the words that have been given to me and through me in whatever manner that can be.

There are a lot of differing styles and types of poems in the book but that is largely due to them being chronologically out of place and because they represent the mood and learning of Christian life that's taken place in me and the way that some of the words have come to me. Some have appeared to me to be very difficult and sombre but that's probably part of the direction, who knows, maybe there is a need to think for a moment or two for a reflection on life and the way that all of our lives are going.

My personal direction is always surprising me, I started on the ECLF (Exploring Christian Life and Faith formally the Ministry Foundation course) late in 2002 and also I started to read books by Phillip Yancey.

Both have been making a profound effect on me as the course has brought to me the need to read the Bible, but also with like minded people, and Phillip Yancey has brought to me the need to communicate with others the words and the love of the Jesus we aspire to in ways that are given to us and not to be shy or too modest about a gift that you may have, it is God given and deserves to be shared.

I was a bit worried initially because the poems and the verse that I will be sharing with you in this book are often personal experiences, so personal sometimes that you will wonder if you should share them with any one. I have often had that dilemma, what will I be thought of if I reveal this or that?. The Jesus we know and love did so and he was crucified for his openness and his love for all.

But learn from the reasons, look at how he was betrayed for it was not only Judas, but the jealousies of the world and all around Him. Make no mistake, it was this, his great message that we need to understand and realise that although we are individuals, we are all part of His great family and loved by the Father through Jesus. This concept was difficult for me to grasp and I still find a great deal of difficulty sometimes just contemplating that very ideal.

Anyway, to make a start on the book overall is to start by introducing a poem, and it's an early one, one written around the September 11th 2001 attack, a poem that was written as a result of that awful terrorist atrocity. As I said above, it defies comprehension and description, but it shows what is possible when belief becomes fundamentalistic, to the point that the recipients of the wrath are not even considered, or if it is, then it's a legitimate target of the "cause". I have tried very hard to understand the reasons and why we find ourselves doing such things, but to no avail, so this poem is the reaction that I had to the twin towers tragedy.

I say tragedy, for it was just that, nothing was gained from that evil event, and though the misguided will say that there is a message there, look keenly at what has happened and is in fact happening since, reflect on it.

David Cope

September 11ᵗʰ 2001

What was it on that fateful day, what was it in their minds all say,
The world would never be the same, the joy the power an end it came.
They left their lairs and hunted near, they laid a trail forever fear.
For God and for the leader's word, the death the hurt would be for ever heard.

It was for him who had a mind, the wish to end a race he felt unkind,
But does he know what he unfolds, the wakening fear the hatred moulds;
His bestial act will start a swell, that soon will bring us all so close to hell,
The many people he has brought to fear, will forever have in eye a tear.

How can you try to quell a world, with death and mayhem crudely hurled.
Yes kill the unbeliever over there, kill the Christian any time or where,
Whose belief does this for mortal men, that asks for killing oh yes again.
The towers construed like Babel high, but who should say who'll live or die.

Does love of God mean we should kill, and yet for him we always will!
The Lord of Holy Almighty One, he hears our words and soon they're gone.
Hear them now they know more than you, their way is wrong it's right we do!
We are the chosen ones of God, we shall be victors use Moses rod!

And so the biggest highest of mans world, is of a story that was soon unfurled,
But was it right to take those lives, the men the children and someone's wives?
Use any means to say I'm right, no need to worry we can soon fight,
Kill them in the name of faith, the threat of death the bloody wraith.

Until the world can see the light, then we will always always fight,
To get our side across to those, who cannot see what's in this prose;
The futile plea the words we say, can we get to the ones that plotted for that day?
No is the answer they are too deep, to hear the word, the Lord who'll softly
weep.

21.09.01

4

We often ask ourselves about God. What is he (or she) like, what is the reason that God seems to be distant and out of sight and out of hearing. We all hear that God loves us for what we are, so why doesn't God show that we mean so much to Him?

Well the answer is very much in our own hands I suspect, do we go to Him or do we reject Him. Do we only ask where He is when we're in trouble? Have you ever stopped and thought about that wayward brother or sister or relative, who only comes around when they're in a mess. What do you think? Oh no, not so and so again. Well God doesn't, but you have to admit that it's a good point, why should He help when all the time we don't want Him around us, don't want to be encumbered by the rules and regulations that is part of this "God" thing.

Lets take this 'family approach' which is where we seem to start with Gods family, when we all come home and rejoice in the family we are and share, but doesn't that have squabbles? How often have you had the most idyllic week end or Christmas with the family when something starts to happen and the peace is totally shattered!! How many break ups occur at Christmas, Easter, holiday times, why?

Well like a lot of people, I've contemplated this a lot and I suspect strongly that this is where our free will comes in, and the freedom to choose what we do, who we like and how we want our lives to be.

We search for the elusive "happy" life, but how do you see that, and how do you go about getting it?
The fundamental issue here is our selfishness our free will taking over, for I want this or that and my way is right. Or is it? Did I think about what I just said, did it offend and did I express my wishes in a sensible and constructive way, are my wants and desires right and reasonable?

Taking the lack of understanding and our free will a stage further, what happens when the problem escalates to the level of a nation taking issue? We go to war!, and as we know war doesn't just start, there are preliminaries and the way to it often is tracked by history and justified as being necessary or for a good reason. How often do the common people get a chance to contribute, other than to lose their lives in a conflict that often defies all sense and reason.
Look through the centuries at the wars we've had, and don't merely take the worn old record and say "Bigger and greater wars have been fought in the

name of religion", we fought them, not God, although we all say that He's on "our side" don't we. Well in a way He is, because He overlooks all that we do, but our free will dictates the way that we make our lives and the way we take them. God gives us the life we have, but the way that we lose the struggle of our lives is more to do with our own will than with what God provides.

Where is this all going? Well it runs to the next poem, the futility of the conflict of war. Imagine the way it comes about? I have a fascination about the First World War, probably because my maternal grandfather was involved in it and although he wasn't killed during it, it is arguable that the after effects had a direct bearing on his untimely demise at the age of forty seven. The fact is that the First World War was devastatingly costly in the amount of killing that went on. The trenches and the charges across no man's land, the way that these days it's analysed in how many were killed and the tactics of the battles. It's of no comfort to a family who loses a loved one how the tactics ran, and how good the generals or commanders were, the stark truth of it all is that we lose the ones we love. As I say my family was touched by the loss of a father, not directly in the war but as a consequence of the methods used.

Imagine the soldier who has left his home and loved ones, gone to do his duty for a cause that seems to have been right, and then the unimaginable happens, well read the poem and tell me what you'd be thinking as death overtook. Imagine the Christ as He faces the final battle that He must, for us and for the Father.

War: A soldier

Upon a distant battlefield he lay there dying,
cursing his lot, the pain wracks his body, listen he's crying.
How did he get here, why does he lie low
as his mind starts to wander, he's not long to go.

His mind now plays tricks and he cannot see straight,
he thinks for a moment he's homeward and almost quite late.
The train whistles loudly and on it did leap,
the lads hurry homeward for their women folk weep.

Suddenly he's back home with his family his children, his wife;
the home he had worked for, would defend with his life.
He sees his young daughter the apple of his eye,
she runs to her daddy the love is so clear, the question now's why.

The babe in the parlour the one crying now
is the son that he prayed for, the one that he loved so and how.
His house is so perfect and so beautiful, take a look here,
the whole of his life was so perfect, it was ever so clear.

But now look at him, dying his life shattered there,
a poor local peasant is standing nearby, just giving a stare.
Remind me what was he doing here, what was the grand plan?
But listen, It's all for the best friend, he's helping some man.

He looks down at his comrades those lying nearby
he can't even give them a friendly goodbye.
They were killed day's before he received this last shot
the one that has killed him and decided his lot.

God's with us they claimed as they marched off to war
but what is the reality of the carnage, the killing, what was it for?
They say it's a must that we defend us from them
but who say's that to oblivion this man we condemn?

His mind although reeling is back in the field
his life now is draining and it shortly must yield,
to this bloody insane conflict that he's been drawn in.
oh Lord will you tell us why we all think we'll win?

David Cope

And so through the ages we kill for the cause
and never for a moment to consider or pause
"the Lord is on our side" is our battle cry friend
the enemy is out there and to hell them we'll send.

What of the son or the father just there?
is he the enemy or a friend, should we care?
before you condemn him to die, take his life
remember our dear Christ for he took all our strife.

Think of the mother who stood 'neath the cross
what was her thought of this the great earthly loss,
the Father who knew what was happening here,
the ultimate sacrifice of his own son so dear.

And even though our saviour was broken and slain
from his obedient passion we should all gain
the futility, the obstinate thoughts of mere men
who think we should kill for peace, but God asks us when?

21st October 2001

I actually saw a very long film about the American Civil war some time ago, something that I knew very little about other than it was about slavery and cotton!. How wrong could I be, but it brought home the futility, the humanness of such conflicts and the bestiality of the treatment of each for the other and in the context too of a civil war.

Yet even in that awful bloody conflict there were times of great giving and sharing, sacrifice for each other. At a time when the world seemed to have gone completely mad, there appears the body of Christ there working away and making sense of this otherwise senseless existence.

Going on from the American Civil war and the civil war's that we still have, ours in the 1640's and the American civil war in the 1860's of which much was written and many poems came about, we can look to the 1930's and the Spanish civil war which created a movement that endures to this day. Many have heard of and indeed participated in, "Cursillo", which comes as a gift from the Spanish and the Roman Catholic Church, but is a gift that all Christians would do well to consider.

It is in simple terms a short course for Christians to take, over three days to re-affirm and to further their faith. You will see references to Cursillo in this book, and I make no apology for that, as I and my wife have been on a Cursillo week end (and been privileged to staff too) and know what it is capable of. One of the best aspects of the movement is that it produces what is called the "Fourth Day Community" which is in fact following the course, the rest of your life, but in the "Fourth Day" Community there exists a real opportunity for dedicated Christians to affirm and confirm their faith and do something for Christ. Sunday Christians are OK, but the real need is for the Evangelisation that Christ meant us to do on His behalf, but to do it for Him and through Him, not for us or by us but being the body of Christ here on earth. The only way that He can communicate positively is through you and me I'm afraid, we have to motivate ourselves to "spread the gospel" for him. This is why He chose disciples and this is why we get chosen too, sometimes without really knowing it!

Part of the participation on these Cursillo weekends is to give prayer gifts, called "Palanca". There will be some of those in here, simple but meant for the day to day living in the world that God gave us, to keep us going and to keep our souls near to Him.

The fact is a friend of ours, Phillip Orme was Lay Rector at a recent Cursillo in the Leicester Diocese (Number 19 in May 2003) and there was an opportunity to send such "gifts". Here is one of them:

Let God take your hand

Firmly - gently - guided for the Love of others; for the Love of you - the whole of creation.

Guide you, keep you as you give to others, of you, of the Godliness in you - the spirit of the Lord working through you.

Gently speak in His name, loudly call our Alleluia as you proclaim His greatness, His humbleness, His gift.

His Son - for He is with you, and me and all of us, this day and ever more.

Hosanna - He Lives

FOR US!

The amount of friends we have been blessed with through Cursillo is amazing, but then that's what Jesus meant for us. To be a family in His name, and to be His body on earth.

I mentioned earlier that I started off in September 2002 when I embarked on the ECLF (Exploring Christian Life and Faith formally the Ministry Foundation course) course which I completed in June 2003 and I was wondering just where I'm going next. There was plenty of fun and much debate during this package, and I made a couple of very good friends too, but it is all for the growing of our faith and spirituality, or so I'm told, and I was clear that I must keep my head in my Bible. Problem is that I started to read some books that rather diverted me from my main purpose, but they've actually acted as a catalyst and made me look at 'me' again.

I first saw Phillip Yancey's books in a Christian book shop in Royal Leamington Spa.
It was on the way home from a glorious week on the canals. A week alone with my wife, one of those weeks of glorious togetherness we often lose sight of in this busy busy world of ours.
It was very odd that as I walked into the shop, Gen, my wife asking me "What book do you fancy getting?" that I was drawn to one book, which I bought, that being "Reaching for the Invisible God". It was rather appropriate at the time too, since I was on one of my "Where's my real faith" downers. I'm prone to these and I can be very down when dogged by them, so the inspiration from this book was all the more remarkable, but so much a book that I really couldn't put it down. I'd really recommend it to anyone who is struggling to find God in this tough old world of ours. So you'll probably find that it's strange that it's not that book that I am referring to now. In fact it is a Philip Yancey book, but this particular one is "Finding God in Unexpected Places".

The reason I looked into this book was not only the fact it was Phillip Yancey, but also and mainly as it happened, there was a chapter called "Finding God on the Job". This was all because at this time I was working miles away from home and I suppose I was looking for a sort of God experience to help me get through the wearisome days, not only working, but travelling the 70 miles or so that I was doing everyday going to and from work. So, again, you will find it odd that I'm not referring to this chapter either!!. So what am I up to? Answers on a plain post card to "Confused Christian Hollycroft Hinckley".

Seriously though, it was as I read this book that some parts of it became so important to share that I just had to do that. The strange bit is that it's about the former USSR. It was chapter 21, "Russia's Untold Story" that started me off and I was so intrigued. Yancey talks about the sudden demise of the Communist state and the effects of that, and moving from an atheist state overnight to probably the hugest mission possibility in the world. He talks of a person whom he met whilst visiting Russia some time ago and how this man had been imprisoned for his faith and how he had set up a Church when it was not the right thing to do in Russia (or USSR as it was then known). Yancey goes on to describe the visit to Russia in some detail and how he and other Christian delegates were to be guests at the Journalists club in Moscow. He talks of the challenge they expected as they talked about Christian ethics and what difference Christianity would make to Russia in these new times.

They had a shock, a huge shock for they asked for help on forgiveness, and the Christian way. The day after this meeting they were visiting the Academy of Social Sciences, which is or was a finishing school for Marxist/Leninist leaders. What a challenge. These are those who had lived the dream of the communist way, a very hard bitten regime having had many years of indoctrination of the communist ethics. The comment that came from this meeting and explained by Yancey was that they knew the dream was over and they wanted to move towards "Liberal Democracy", but that they didn't know how, they no longer knew what values to build society upon.

This in itself put a huge image in my mind, not just the Russian people's future and their problem of grasping the Christian way, but just a little bit of our culture sparked in my mind and I began to search my soul about the reality of how our world is going.

Yancey includes an excerpt from the speakers that they encountered at this Academy and that one speaker says that we need no God to have morality, and that Lenin and Marx made mistakes but that their socialist vision is fine and that Christianity had been tried in Russia for a millennium, without success in their view. The response to this was fairly lengthy but the man who spoke from the Yancey's delegation again reminded me of my own deepest thoughts. He said that he had times of doubt and that he'd read Dostoevsky's novel "The Brothers Karamazov". He started to lose his faith as he saw the sincerity and the arguments against God given by the one brother. He was eventually won over to God by the other brother who showed love. The atheist had fine arguments but lacked that which only God can give, the truest love of all.

The final part although by no means the end of the experience of this wonderful book, is the comments about the "God that Failed". Yancey explores the God whom the communists replaced our God with. That of man, who was held to be the equal. That in essence seemed OK but the communists ignored the most fundamental part of the whole point of the love of God. That is our fallen nature for we do not have the capacity or the breadth of love and the ability to understand our nature and to forgive. We need to look at our world and we should not condemn or be above ourselves. Look at who Jesus himself worked and lived amongst, and who he forgave and who he befriended, and then consider whom it was that condemned and arranged his execution.

This book is clearly a wonderful experience and makes us look carefully at the world we are in. Yancey's book tells us a further comment by the Russians about the Marxist experiment, they refer to the seventy four years on the road to nowhere. I wonder if we are any better in the morals and high ground we take?. I wonder?. Mentioning love and how that is around us and with us, the next poem is something of the way that I tried to envisage the way that God loves us, unequivocally.

Love

Love is from the Lord, and Love is for the Lord;

We cannot conceive the breadth and depth of Love that He holds for us.

We are to Him as shallow as a Pool of water:

We aspire to His great Love and mirror Him as minute ripples in the reflected face of some small pool of spiritual faith, disturbed by dreams of faith as pebbles cast into the greatness of His eternal spiritual pool.

His greatness is beyond our comprehension, beyond our faith, beyond us in entirety, and yet His greatness is bestowed upon us individually, before -- during -- and after our mortalness is conceived and known then left.

21st February 2003

What are you like on words? A proper crossword buff or real brainiac where words are concerned? Well there is a word, "interregnum", what is that? Well I thought about the English civil war, there being an interregnum then, between Kings so to speak. Well you get these when your Vicar/Rector your local parish priest moves on. It sounds like a disease and to be honest it feels like it when you start the process of trying to find another member of the clergy to lead your Church. Not only that, where Gen and I worship we're in a Benefice of 5 Churches so you have five times the "process".

Despite being Anglicans we all have different ways to worship and we all have differing ways of how we feel that should be done. It's a great pity that the energies we expend in our differences aren't used to extol our similarities, things would be a lot easier and we'd find our way sooner and with much less trial and tribulation. Of course we have traditional things we carry and we have the legacy of how we did it umpteen years ago. But then we have the younger folks, who don't have all that and want something from Christianity that they don't know sometimes, and can only see what we make of it, the old ones who are trying to come to terms with the fact we are getting old!. But of course we've got all that baggage and years of prejudices about this and that, we can't just open up, can we, to a possible different approach, we think that we've got it right and that change is not inevitable.

The problem is that it's not actually change, it's in fact making the relevance of Jesus in our lives in the context of the times we live in. Also can younger folks relate to that? Bearing in mind that a lot of younger folks don't have the benefit (or otherwise) of the teaching either from school or the family, about Church and Christianity, the fact is that although technology has zoomed into the 21st Century, poor little man in the street is still the frightened, insecure, unsure or happy go lucky whatever, individual they always were, only now we have the trappings of the age we live in.

I dare say that in 100 or 1000 years from now, the speculation will still be the same, and people will still write about the same things we've all done over the centuries. But God's message will still hold as true then as ever it does now, or when the old Testament was formed or when Jesus started His ministry. Will we still have the Churches as we know them today? Will we still pray and will Jesus have come again by then? Who know's?

A good time for a poem, what do you think? Well it's my book so I suppose it's up to me anyway: I wrote this poem as I wondered about Jesus and thought would any of us recognise Him if we met Him, well you judge.

A City Street

Along a city street I walked one night, a wet and windy autumnal night,
chilling to the bone.
I crossed a road and saw the shining lights reflected in the rain: I felt so
lonely as along I strode, shrugging off the rain and biting wind. But then I
heard a voice a man who walked behind me called to slow my pace.

I wondered what it was he wanted, but out of some simple inner feeling, I
slowed down to match his slower pace.
His face was tanned and did not fit the cold and wet of English autumn
time, he looked so out of place. Then we walked together at a much much
slower pace, and chatted freely, strangely like old friends, about anything
and everything, but almost in a knowing way.

We trod the highway wet with rain and came upon a dark and dingy street,
I felt my heart just skip a beat, but somehow the man I'd met just walked
on as normal, never faltered just onward stepped he did.

I said to him did he feel the same and all he said was "Keep with me I have
a journey that is never to be feared". The light was poor and rain now fell in
torrents, wetting us until it ran in rivulets down our very backs.

I felt the pace had quickened but had it really? I looked at him and asked
politely if we walked much quicker now, never was a word he spoke he
merely smiled and on we went.

I felt so much better now though even wet and cold, no longer miserable as
we strode our sodden path. But then we reached the fork where our roads
must part, the road where I must walk to find my way back home.

He looked along the path that lay quite opposite to mine, and again he
smiled as right along he walked. I waved to him and wished him well and
asked how far was home for him.
He smiled again, a smile I could not take my eyes from easily, he said
goodbye and then he whispered so very quietly to me as along his way he
walked.

"My journey's long and down so many paths with you, and many paths
with all who heard my call to them, my home is far but near you see, and

you will one day know it for yourself, but till that day remember our meeting and how we talked and how the rain no longer mattered".

Then into the rainy night I saw not where he went but all these days I'll follow in those footsteps, now and evermore.

13th September 2003

Chapter Two
Where on Earth am I Going?

Ever found yourself in a situation and thought "How the heck did I get into this lot!". Or some such wording, a place where you wonder what your purpose is and why the need is for you particularly to be there. Well go on, have you? I bet you have and I bet that you still don't really know the answer to it either.

Well as a small child I was a bit of a dreamer, still am in fact. Mum used to worry like mad about the fact that I spent more time dreaming than in the real world. Kids are good at that, the problem is that some of us don't grow out of it, and that causes all sorts of problems. The next poem is reminiscent of those childhood days, when my brothers thought I was daft and probably still do, but I loved the dreams, I still do, for in them the world is OK, the way to God is so easy, no PCC (Parochial Church Council) meetings, no worries about if you're a Roman Catholic, Anglican, Methodist or whatever. You can be just you and the whole world is at peace with you and that very thought that you hold.

Dreaming Again!

I'm dreaming, drifting off again as I often do,
I'm just that kid again, the knight with maids to woo.
Was I seven or eight or ten? Well whatever age I start to dream again.
I dream of many childish things and blot out any pain.

I dream of dragons wizards and the like
And wonder if I'll ever get that smashing bike;
But then I drift into the world of forests fields and streams,
And I can see so clearly there all manner in my dreams.

The trees I see as a breeze blows through,
And little birds sing softly there as they often do;
I hear my little brother cry, he often breaks my dream;
And then my mother comforts him and off again I dream.

Now where was I then, I broke the dream I had,
And if I can't return to it I really will be sad.
The childish mind seeks out their roles as only children can;
Then as if by magic in their minds there starts this special man.

I suddenly become a man, the greatest man of all,
And even though I can't quite see his face I know I'll never fall.
Throughout the land I roam around and everyone loves me;
And even though I'm far away they always seem to see.

I try again to see this face, this man for all the land,
I think of him and try again his power it's so grand.
Around the world I travelled far the people always glad
And if someone was crying there I'd stop them being sad.

It's such a shame that we grow up and lose these childish dreams,
For in the story here there are the real life themes;
I know I was a part of Christ, His body here on earth;
And even though I didn't know it then I loved with all I'm worth.

My prayer is to be with Him still as around the earth He'll go,
And to those who need the most our smiling faces show.
So as the child who dreams his dreams for Christ will use us all,
Don't forget as you grow up, just dream and dream, then listen for His call.

8th May 2002

19

You see that your childhood shapes you in more ways than you perhaps realise and we also pick up most if not all the "baggage" that we cart around with us for the rest of our lives. Jesus hands us many offers in the Bible to "let go" to follow Him and be a Disciple, but how often do we truly follow His lead? I suppose that we can't all do that because He wants us to be His creation and we are actually all created differently and that's why He loves us so much. Because we are all the same as humans, but in our manner we can be miles apart, heaven and earth apart, doesn't make anyone wrong, just His children, different and individual but in His image.

So back to this question, where am I going? Well I suppose that my life as a Christian is too long and tortuous to go into here, maybe another book one day perhaps, but I need to say that I came back to the Church after my Dad died, a proper Christian that is (and in fact whatever that means!). Common enough sort of thing, loads of folks suddenly find the need to go to Church when a trauma hits the family. Then of course, once you get there, there's the ones that say, "well now would you like to do something for the Church". At this point is it the polite refusal or "I'm not going back there because I don't want to do anything, it's not my scene", situation. Well I've been there like many, and have you found out, you can turn your back, you can shun it all, but one day you'll find that you become involved, it gets you!.

Dads passing was apart from anything else, odd in a way because I never felt that I grieved for him, not especially, but then Dad and I were never that close, or were we? It was not until my Mother died that I started to realise a lot of things about him and of course Mum. She hated the growing old part of life and maybe although I'd had a healthy respect for Christianity all my life, I never really started to question until the real mortality of us all struck me and Mums words came rolling back after she had passed away from us.

I talked earlier on about Cursillo, this short course in the Christian faith; well in some way that was my "doing" or "undoing" whichever view point you come from. I have to say that I always knew that deep down I would get involved in some fashion although like anything to do with God, you never know until "His will be done!". Then you've no choice but it's not being coerced, it's not being railroaded, it's not being forced, you seem to come to terms with the fact that Jesus said that we would be His body on earth, and we have to do His work as His body on earth and there you suddenly find yourself doing it.

I well remember my younger brother saying about my move back to the Church, "Its' because you're getting old, you want to get your card stamped". Well he could be right of course, but I'm not that sure really because I suppose that I have become painfully aware of my advancing years and the fact that both Genesta and I have been married 37 years this year (Married 27.06.70) which brought home the realisation of that fact, so much so that I penned a few words on that very subject, then I'd better get back to the original point about how we get where we are! So with Mums words in mind and my own thoughts on the 'getting old!' the next poem sort of fell into place so to speak.

Age

Why do we age, what is it for?
The culmination of a lifelong tour.
Each wrinkle line and crows foot shows,
the ever increasing amount of daily blows.

It starts as just a little laughter line;
No need to worry yet no need to whine;
But as the years go swiftly by
The more you cover them but try.

You look back wistfully at the shot,
They took of you, Oh the looks you'd got;
The childish impish ways of then,
Come flooding back to you again.

I did not change I hear you say,
It was just the years, Oh yesterday;
The joy of youth the way we were,
Oh pity now just look at her.

The road is narrow short, one way;
I can take it all, the twists, the turns, I hear you say;
But when upon the threshold standing there,
The final straight you stand and stare.

The short leap from our childhood years,
The path we trod and all the fears;
Completed now in grandest splendour,
But the ageing of us all is the offender.

Beyond this toil we have on earth,
Will prove to be of greater worth;
When stand before the greatest one,
The shackles, wrinkles, lines, will all be gone.

14th January 2002

Something you'll also note in this book are that the dates of the poems flit all over the place, that's because they seem to be fitting into this book better in this way rather than merely doing them in strict chronological order.
It seemed a bit clinical too, just to drop them into a strict order and try and make sense of them by doing that.

So to the point, again! "how the heck did I get into this lot". Well I have some very good friends in the Church, (mind you that's a debateable point!) and when you get the times that faith seems to desert you and you wonder why things happen in a certain way, they step in and all of a sudden you find a load of things going on that you didn't realise that you agreed to.

Like the fact that we started to go to a local Church, in a village just across the way from the estate which we live on and within the twinkling of an eye I became a Church Warden. Now bearing in mind that I'm a local councillor, and at that time I was working a fair distance way from home, and I like to write poems and research family history, how on earth was I going to find the time to do this as well as everything else.

Well I didn't and to an extent I still don't, and I get stomach troubles through the worry about what I don't do and if I do things well and so on, but someone sees me through it all, good people at church provided by whom?. It might just be those 'friends' and also there could be the strength of the good Lord Himself when we all need Him.

Just flitting back to the 'dreaming days', I had thought that I would live my life quite easily gently and without worries, how many folks do you know that try to do that, then the problems start to arrive. Who do you turn to when the troubles start? Some go to their family, friends, the church, God Himself. How do you approach that? How do you talk to God?
Prayers are a bit naff in today's society until that big tragedy hits your life, how many times do you hear "Oh God!" or "Why me God?", a big question and a question that may well be there all your lives, but why do people call out to a God whom many don't believe in and hardly seek Him out in the good times to say "Thanks".

I'm as guilty as most, I have been elated by his goodness that I can feel tangibly and I am hurt and angry when God seems to turn His back on me, and why? I go to church every Sunday, and I'm doing all these good things for Him, but for the answers, I needed to go to the Bible, there's a bit about Job who was a real God groupie and look at how God served him. So even if you

23

David Cope

take the reins that God passes to you, however that may be, don't expect that the path will be easy, Jesus said that being a Christian would never be easy, but we need to listen and be His children and walk that path.

So walk that path with me a few yards, or even a mile or so, but see if you can feel the way we must go.

Faith - a Journey

I'd stood upon a rise on top of yonder hill, I looked before, blindly but the
air so clear and still;
The path that lay before me now unclear, but it seemed so real and easy, did
I need to fear?:

I trod the ground and felt the earth, my feet were firm and stable there I felt
eternal worth:
The first few stumbling steps I took, the fears the fumbling, my sinful body,
faith and heart all shook:

A revelation came a beautiful appealing path ahead, I leapt for joy I sang
the song, along the path I sped:
The path it was a wondrous way, I sang I praised I sought the Lord I
thought His word I'd always think and say:

Then into gloom I trod naive so clearly unaware, I felt the ground that
heaved my way unclear, did anyone still care?
Then thorns and prickles they pierced my flesh my feet, I cried and called
out Lord!! where is His voice so sweet?.

Suddenly I could not hear I could not feel; the ground so hard, the pain,
the path so hard how could this way be real?
Then shone a light as once before; but different, it cleared my way my path
it cleansed the painful dusty bloodied floor.

I came around a corner in my weary route, I gazed upon the bloodied feet
and saw a ragged some how familiar suit:
And still I couldn't see, perceive this Holy view, But as I strode a cooling
balm upon my feet was from the early dew.

I climbed a tree to see my way; but mist obscured the way ahead, I felt a
sudden fear perhaps the path I'd stray:
But yet again upon the road I stride, the feeling in my heart and soul again
the one I thought had died:

It surged and made my soul a fire, this walk, this path, this pain, from
striding forth to God I knew I'll never ever tire:
My eyes cleared now as on a meadow I espied; a narrow way that looked so
right but worn by countless feet that tried;

25

I forced my way through brambles, thorns and weeds; my naked flesh was
ripped and torn the sweating body bleeds:
Upon a ragged hillside up I climbed; I searched horizon wide and far to
find an easy route, to see a way defined;

I pushed, I prayed, a bush moved clear; I blinked and stared and almost
shrank away in my mortal fear;
Where was I now? what had my eyes revealed, I looked around my cuts my
bruises my aching body healed:

Upon the hillside all in order there, three rough and wooden crosses stood,
I had to stop and stare;
The ills, the blood, my aching heart and soul; all nailed upon a blazing
cross of light I saw complete perfection whole.

Then a hand so softly touched me, lifted up my human form and filled my
searching soul you see;
This hand had beckoned often on the road I'd walked; and now I know
His voice, Lord Jesus in my soul has talked.

8th June 2003

I suppose that fancy words written down and then related, can make a person feel good, spiritual, elated all sorts of emotions but are they getting any nearer God? Do the words actually do any good? I sometimes feel that the kind of books I read and in fact this book, will appeal to a particular type of person and they will read it and hopefully enjoy sharing with me what I have found. But there are those who will look and say to themselves or out loud, another God buster or another load of old !!! well need I go on?.

So why write words that I know will only get to those who will pick the book up because they search, or need, or who are genuinely wanting to get nearer to God, to Jesus to the way He wanted for us. Just think then, you are not the audience I'm actually writing for! Give this book to that other person who doesn't believe, go on do it now. No because you and I both know what would happen don't we (or do we?).

The fact is that it's you and me that need to express these words, fire us up and then tackle the others. Not by going head on, that never has, nor ever will work. We all know that very well! Ask any Jehovah's Witness where their Watchtower magazine gets put these days is down right awful!. Funny thing is that the Church of England spends time losing folks and the splinter groups go round recruiting them. Why is this? Well part of the problem is image and the way that we are. Do we in the Church of England really welcome and help folks to understand what it is we love about Church?, some do but there are those that need to look at themselves very carefully to answer that question.

Anyway, here's a personal question!!! how old are you? An impertinent question but, be honest, in actual yearly terms? I'm 58'ish (early 2007) and rapidly approaching 25!!. The fact is that we age in the body, it falls to bits, but our minds, our ways, how are they?

My mum was around 75'ish when she died but she was still a youngster at heart and very much in her mind, that's how we can be and should be, forgiving and sharing; but bearing in mind our human side how well do we fare on that? Ever been lonely in a crowd? Some of my most lonely times, and unforgiven times have been experienced in a crowd.

People being people we are quite different, we need to be for the sake of mankind, wouldn't be much point if we were all the same would it? And God didn't make us with free will to be all the same, but we are sometimes too different to communicate. History is full of prima donnas and the great artists that must have been hell to live with let alone work with! Why is that?

- Some of the greatest talents that ever lived died early and were completely impossible to live with. It is often said about the 'artists' and the way they are, they seem to be set aside and too difficult!. The average man or woman who is merely the "salt of the earth", get on with life and are "average". What is it that makes these distinctions and why?

In fact the biggest rows and the greatest problems are more about that "character" clash than anything, especially at work and any situation where competitiveness comes in. Those who are single minded "go getters" upset the mild emotional ones and the view is always totally opposite when you discuss these differing folks. Take the great composer Richard Wagner for instance, he wrote arguably, some of the most powerful music ever, not agreed by all but to a real fan he's the tops! But look who favoured him immensely, one of the most reviled men in all of history – Adolf Hitler! – Where is the sense in that?

The fact is if Jesus himself walked through the door this very day, would you recognise him?
How would you know him from anyone else, all the ones that you don't understand or have a bit of a "problem" with? If you recall the poem "A City Street" there's a bit of a question there for you, but if we think of the lonely bit and being lost in a crowd, well what about being in a wilderness? Time for another poem I think:

The Wilderness

Stood in the middle of nowhere, today, yesterday or was it tomorrow? Was it a field? a desert? what was it I was in? And yet I seem to stand within a thousand people, but still was in a wilderness.

I felt their presence, near and far, I felt their body warmth and yet, I felt no warmth from them which helped me in my heart.

I called to them out loud and asked "where are you going all of you, in this milling crowd so huge?".
But not a word I heard from anyone, it seemed as if I was within them all but somehow distant, very very far.

I trembled and a tear upon my face did run, I called again but no one answered, no one spoke. I looked to see their faces, a hundred thousand bodies there, but could I see them? what was on their face their brow?

I watched as if transfixed upon this heaving mass, this huge and milling swollen body of humanity, mankind. I peered so hard and then I saw a glowing face, as if a lantern just turned on, shining in this moving mass.

And then, another and another, Oh Joy many could I see -- I saw at once that we all walked towards the same eternal way.

I heard their call, the same as mine, I knew that I had not been all alone, just blinded by this grey and solidness that moved so slow, so deliberately.

I watched afar again as if the world was here before the eyes of those who shone; And there beyond the dark horizon of this wilderness, this mass, this living wilderness of human kind that rolled along without direction, without so much as hope upon their lips.

There a light that shone so bright for those who saw and looked beyond.

A desert holds so many things and reeks of that which often represents to us the worst of what we fear; but deep within its sands, its brush, the life is there it soars above the heat and cold the lack of rain, the inhospitable, that heat that cold that loneliness, that deserts are we're told.

Tell me just how often do we stand within the air conditioned, heated, cos-
 seted, this land of plenty, given by the Hand and modified by man?.

How often do we stand just there and stand within a wilderness of man
a wilderness we make, a wilderness more terrifying than the desert which
holds the key; a story told to tell us all, it says that we should look and see;

Where is that wilderness?, that tower of Babel? that place of all temptation?

Read the signs and see the wilderness which within you stand.

12ᵗʰ March 2004

You see we all have our ways and we all think that we're right, I have had huge self confidence problems in my life so I'm always asking if what I did was right, and then when I feel confident, putting my foot in it and then having an awful time afterwards anguishing about why I did it wrong.

So I feel lonely sometimes, because I don't feel that I'm with the "crowd", and then joyfully I see those wonderful Godly people who are shining, on the path of the spirit and forgiving me for what I am.

I mentioned a little way back about Jesus walking through the door and would we recognise Him, well in the poem "On a City Street" it talks about meeting a stranger on that city street and who was He?
Also did I communicate with Him? How well do I communicate with others? How well do you? The problem is not only are there language barriers to encounter, there's also emotional and character barriers that set us a million miles apart.

Jesus could communicate with all and to all, and still does! But we struggle with the words left behind because all we can do is read and then interpret those words as best we can using the intellect or understanding available to us in whatever end of the scale in life we find ourselves in, and that can lead to all sorts of identity problems as we find a problem with trust, because we start to suspect why this person says or does this or that. Jealousy is a threat because we feel that we're as good as this or that person, and you are, but not in the same way or at the same things. What we need is to be able to identify what we're good at and see where that falls with others so together we work constructively in His grace.

Many of the poems I've written look at and talk about the identity of Christians and the way we are meant to work together in Jesus' name. We all do in a fashion but it can be hard work. Strong wills and forthright attitudes can be hurtful and seen as an obstruction. We none of us progress, live, or grow spiritually at the same pace so those who move quickly or lead for instance find it difficult to countenance the "lesser mortals" which can lead to hurt, damaging of faith and sometimes complete rejection.
And again the baggage that we've carried with us over the years can be apparent in the way we react and respond.

Reflect on the words:

What was Said

Take a look at you, take a look at me,
What was in your hearts your eyes, what was it you could see?

I stood and looked straight at your face,
and you looked straight at me, was there honesty and grace?
What welled up in your heart,
Think a moment, touch the Christ, where did that thinking start?

You disagreed but couldn't hear,
What was it then that someone said, speaking without fear.

I speak too blunt for you he said,
And when the words all tumbled out, his tongue had weaved a thread.

Did you listen to what you spoke,
Could you hear what they just said, their meaning in a cloak?

Would you say to Jesus near,
What you just said to all, when you said you had no fear.

When you speak your mind,
Remember if you're right and good or are those words unkind?

And are they really true?
Or are they coming from within, a twisted unclear view?

What did James declare,
About your tongue, the restless evil deadly poison there.

Love abounds where love is real,
Come to fellow men, and hold the hand, then the Lord you'll feel.

2nd February 2004

Being as the Church needs good people so much many are drawn in to help and "do", and this can be very beneficial to some, but down right disastrous to others. The journey we're all on is a difficult one and our talents are often misconstrued as are our characters. We expect quite fundamental changes to people and God causes this very often, but we also need to respect the fact that there are those who are as God intended, and at what point is your requirement a demand or an imposition upon what is right already and what God meant to be.

So here we ask ourselves, would we know Jesus and when we're so sure we're right and the other person is anguishing over their point of view too, are we really doing Gods will. Maybe, but pray about that and ask Him, you may do more damage than you realise, ask yourself this question:

The Question?

The question was asked, were you there when they crucified my Lord?

Who was it in those long passed days who uttered each immortal word?

How many times in your life have you stood and watched someone crucified?

Was it because you did nothing, stared on, or because you lied?

As Peter denied his Lord 3 times over and cried bitterly after,

Can you hear them now, all those who would do the same, their laughter?

To stand by and do nothing, evil triumphs over good,

But to take the cross and march with Christ, if you could.

No I fear, it's easier each time to stand and stare,

Let them do it now, what can I do should I care?

Yes we were all there when they crucified My Lord

Believe me everyday by deed or thought or word

Yes we all were there when they crucified my Lord.

20th April 2002

Chapter Three
Facing Up to Life?

What are you like with a crisis? Any good, well capable? Fact is I'm not too good at all. I handle them but they drain the stuffing out of me and I feel afterwards that maybe I didn't discharge my duties well but adequately. Confronting our daily duties and the responsibilities of life is a tough one too, I have always had a problem there and that comes from my early days as my Dad pushed us hard as children and ruled with a rod of iron. Quite common amongst post war and "just" pre-war kids I bet, but it's a valid point nevertheless.

I have a habit of worrying and anguishing like mad before an event and then finding it much easier once I'd come to terms with it, and accepting it. Typically there's the hospital appointments, dental appointments, interviews etc etc, and they caused me problems.

I grew up with all this and a very big problem with Dad, basically we never got on at all. When he died suddenly I was undeniably shocked and distressed, but not as grief stricken as I felt that I should have been. I felt inevitable guilt with this and I had a big problem with his passing because not only had we been distant I felt that we were not even close resulting in a difficult childhood and a difficult adolescence.

Dad, I think struggled with this facing of reality too, and he agonised over things which I hadn't thought about until after he died. More latterly as I had decisions of some gravity in my life I pondered on this, and Dad's situation and eventually after much thought on the matter and a number of interesting and thought provoking discussions on the ECLF (Exploring Christian Life and Faith) course I came to write this poem about Jesus, in the garden of Gethsemane. It quite puts my paltry situation into perspective somehow!

Gethsemane

As night draws near and in this place, this garden peaceful for my soul,
He sits and stares above His countenance divine, at where His destiny must
lie.

But as He sits His friends not sure of what the future holds, His mind is
full of what is done and what there is to do.

The evil of the world around, the task that really needs be done, and then
the task before Him lays, the one His Father calls for Him to do.

How many times your father's words have you not heeded though? But this
immenseness of the world before Him lays, the task He must endure.

Be stripped and flogged and awfully defiled before all eyes and everyone,
then nailed upon a cross. Why me? Why now? Will ever this act bring
peace?.

But only the Father and He himself knew well that peace on earth would
never be, but hope would always be, of this we can be sure.

Again reflect as night draws in as betrayed He knows He must; submit be-
fore those the ones who envy, hate despise Him so.

The stillness of the night, the starry sky with peace and tranquil twinkling
nights, a sky so clear as when His birth announced – Yes the coming of a
King the greatest of them all.

Sits now within the tranquil walls, Gethsemane, the garden awaits His final
call, upon the kiss from one who would betray the Son of God for useless
earthly pieces the purchase of His blood His life in monetary terms.

So within the peace the sanctuary of this a gentle quiet place, As with His
conscience He would wrestle and as scripture said and Father did com-
mand, dutifully the Son of God reflects His work on Earth, accepts His call
of everlasting sacrifice.

3rd March 2004

37

This chapter is all about facing up to life, and it's about many things within our lives, but life itself is the problem. I feared death and as I got older became obsessed with what was going to happen on that final day. A bit pointless really because when it arrives, it arrives, and you can worry about it until it finishes you off, or you can accept the teachings of Christ that there is a promise of life to come. You can take the view of many atheists and say "well life just ends". That's the problem too, I can't accept that at all. That's why I've written poems about memories, all that stored up junk in my head and that probably applies to countless others. Fact is why should all that "stuff" just disappear as if it never happened? What would be the point?

I watched a 70's cult sci-fi film again recently, "Blade Runner", it's a futuristic film that is pretty violent, and describes a future that's pretty bleak too, but it deals with a very delicate subject especially these days, that of "Replicants", a sort of "super human robot" just like us but possessing super abilities being genetically engineered "androids" used to work on "off world planets" as a kind of slave labour. They are given a lifespan of only four years, just in case they start to develop feelings or human type traits and try to come to earth (Which is incidentally, forbidden). There are special cops, called Bladerunners who are there to "retire" them if they get above their station and try to return and cause any problems. An actor Rutger Hauer plays one of the most ruthless of a bunch of replicants who return to earth in an attempt to get to their "maker" and increase their life spans. Harrison Ford is the Bladerunner who is enticed out of retirement to track down these particular "replicants" and it is all very bloody as he does so. But at the end of the film the replicant played by Rutger Hauer has almost finished off Harrison Fords character, after a hugely violent number of scenes and they are on the roof of this building and its raining like mad. The replicant realises his time is over and he saves Harrison Ford from sure death and then he comes out with a speech about his memories "lost like tears in the rain" just before he declares "Time to die" and he does so. Good film makers stuff, nice emotional twist to the film but how many people do you know or know of, that died early, from cancer, accidents, heart attacks, war you name it, or those with rich long lives filled with memories and great experiences. How do we feel or think of their times, their emotions some shared with us and some very private, all lost forever, who knows?

Another poem, surprisingly it's just called "Memories";

Memories

All those memories, tears and emotions all lost in time;
All of those words, forgotten that wouldn't rhyme.
Are they forgotten never brought back to life?
All of life's struggles, your particular strife?

What happens to all the emotions you have stored up?
Are they all lost forever like water, that's spilled from an upended cup?
Do you remember your first loving thought?
Everyone should be like that, hadn't they ought?

When all of my memories locked in my head;
Where do they go to when after I'm dead?
Are they lost in the mists of infinity? No one will know,
I cannot believe that, how can they mean nothing and merely just, go?

So where do I go from this spot right now,
I would love to have great faith and call out and how
But I am a sinner who wants to know God;
How can I reach him when minds cluttered with these thoughts, so odd.

I try in these poems to call out to Him,
And make sure my callings are not just a whim,
I call to the Master the King of us all,
The world and me here, Lord we need now Your call.

We kill each and another and reckon without you,
How can we keep clear, the way to the Majesty to your Holy view?.
I have tears in my eyes as I sit here and write;
The thoughts in my mind, the emotions, but I still see the sights!.

Help us dear Master, put into our hearts
The message that everything ends where it all starts
Each and every soul that has lived here,
Has an emotion a feeling so dear.

So why should they be lost for ever I ask?
Who do I call on who'll answer this task?
My heart Lord it bleeds, my eyes filled with tears;
I have such a feeling from the rooftops I'd shout out my fears.

But what is the point of all this feeling inside,
Will it all get washed away Lord and lost with the last tide?
My heart is so heavy, at times I think of my life,
What is the purpose but I still feel a cutting like the blade of a knife.

The cut that wounds deep to my very soul here,
That intrinsic feeling my hollow souls fear;
Our memories and thoughts the essence we are,
Will all be revealed and stored not very far.

They're away from the people that we thought we'd be;
Only to find the Lord's made us see.
But again, I can't see and sometimes feel lost;
And each time I weep Lord I feel, what is this cost?

And what of the ones, the people out there?
Who crush all your good thoughts and don't have a care?
Why should the goodness in them or in here?
Be lost forever, why do I still feel fear?

The mystery of it will, remain till we meet,
The Master of all, the King on His seat.
But now as I grow older, weaker, and fearful in mind
I pray Lord upon us, please help us be kind.

14th April 2002

The funny thing is too that before we leave this part, I realised that the "android" Rutger Hauer, refers to the "tears in the rain", as he makes his poignant little speech which I suppose as I say is all good film making stuff, but it does evoke thoughts about how we cope with life and the way we are, so here is a poem about tears and although I can't say that the film had anything to do with the inspiration for the poem itself, the fact that I was reminded by the film prompts me to include it here:

A Tear

A tear ran down his gentle face, just a tear along His cheek, a wet and
winding trace.
His eyes were misty as His vision saw them gathered all around; with fond-
ness He greets them touches all without a single sound.
His gift of love given to us then, a million times He gives, over and over
and yet again.
His love knows no bounds His gifts ever there; so why do we look so
phased at Him, not seen but forever within His care.
Bruised and battered murdered on a cross, He's always looked out for us,
never as a loss.
Take that tear, wash in it, wash away your fears, Reflect that He's given His
life through a hundred million tears.

The tear runs further down His furrowed face, the toll of years of caring
and giving of His grace.
Imagine wrinkles that adorn His countenance divine, as if each single time
we're hurt, in grief, there cut another line.

His perfect sacrifice is all we need his face a shining glow, there needs no
wrinkle line or mark upon that face to show.

We believe He took the cross, to take the world, its sorrow evil anguish sin
and pain the loss.
To take these from our lives we thought, but never did we realise the words
that He had taught.
We would still have suffering on this earth, but through His sacrifice He
loves us still, because of what we're worth.

31st May 2003

I know of many who would not like this comparison and many who cannot tolerate the emotional side of people. But it exists and it means so much to many of us and in some ways it helps us to handle bereavement, hard times, in fact facing up to the hardships of life. I have, I admit, used my poems to grieve, unload "baggage" to accept life and more importantly in some way, find my faith. Again there is no set way to tackle life and its hardships and the way to faith, just let Jesus lead we will follow but be sure that we do it together and for His glory.

People who are a bit sensitive and prone to being "emotional" or not quite so "tough" as the rest out there often have a tough time handling criticism, or hard comments and the rigours of life that some seem to sail through. Also the things that they do or say and how they do it, can be a real trial for them. It can be a very daunting when you present something which you think is so good, to have someone tell you it's in need of improvement. In reality its quite possibly true and that the tweaking or tuning is not that fundamental, but where the Christian family is concerned trust in their opinions should never need to be questioned for the input or help is offered to improve those efforts not to diminish or destroy them. It's a tough tablet to swallow some times and especially when the greatest effort is put into your "work" if it lacks that extra ingredient that bit that God is trying to make sure you don't leave out, the closest of colleagues seems to be making life intolerable. In truth they're not, it is the body of Christ out there working away again and tolerance is what is needed and that can sometimes be the biggest hurdle, I can say from some bitter experience that this is true.

Relationships, in whatever guise can be something that needs skill and lots of working on and of course plenty of love! Interpretation of what is said, meant, implied are all part of this balancing act of forming and keeping alive relationships and they are part of this very interesting facing up to life. Marriage is typical, as I mentioned earlier, Genesta and I have been married since 1970 (right now at the time of writing this book 2007) it's 37 years ago. Some folks seem to manage only a short time and the marriage goes, why is that? We all have something to say about what goes wrong, is it tolerance? Commitment? Lack of basic trust? Who knows?. Well, we do in a sense, since we first of all look for compatibility and of course if we "fancy" them.

The trouble with that, is after a while, what is the "glue" that joins you together?.

Is it that love, that real love and companionship that joins you together? Just how the Lord Himself suggests. I wrote loads of poems until one day my wife Genesta said "You never write any poems for me".

This was in a way true, but I hadn't really been able to express in a poem what I'd felt. Somehow all the "other" stuff had taken the time and not given me any space for writing this poem. Well I did write one and in fact it's for all couples really. We often have those times when we can't say what we'd like to say, deep down inside and stop it sounding "gushy" and not meaning what you actually want to say, those really deep down words that you can't say. I wanted to say things that were true and yet showed that I was conscious of the fact that our love changed as we changed, as we were together longer we recognised the gift we had been given.

So here's the poem I wrote for Gen, and if it fits for you too, then all the better. It does give me the meaning to the gift of human love that is made for us by the Lord, how we use it and how we share it, that's for us to decide. The important fact is that if we are careful in whom we choose, and then use our tolerance and love, and allow ourselves to grow together in a loving relationship which is as friends too, we will enjoy the fruits of marriage as promised. A bit like how we love Jesus too, growing in our love for Him and His love for us.

Gen's Poem

The love I have the love you are,
The fondness, memories, those days afar;
The coyness of the meeting first,
The love the yearning, youthful thirst.

How could we know what lay ahead,
The world the trials they soon would spread;
But love can hold the spirit firm,
And for each other we'll ever yearn.

The words cannot express in life,
What it has meant to have you wife;
The childishness the youthful blush,
Forever minded our loving rush.

Hold my hand and touch my breast,
Our love is changed but holds the test.;
We stand together through our years
Our love it binds us dissipates the fears.

As long as I am with you in this life,
And loving each the other I fear no strife;
My soul mate, lover wife and friend,
Who but the Maker could He send?.

I loved you then, I love you now,
If only I could give the love my vow;
But as the ages pass and we grow old
The love the burning it goes not cold.

Because our souls, they love as one,
And though those youngsters now are gone;
The man the woman's love will last forevermore,
Because the gift made for us was so sure.

David Cope

Search my soul and see it clear,
I have no reason for to fear;
Reach out and put your hand in mine,
and then our souls will be with Him Divine.
.

31.October 2002

When I wrote this I had a bit of a twinge of conscience about marriage and those folks who choose to live together as partners without the "Churchy" bit. I can't say that I have any problem with that, it's not something I feel qualified to comment on, we didn't do it and I suppose we married very young, we were both 21'ish at the time. But however we have worked on our relationship to the extent that we are as one, we do most things together, we need each other and maybe that's what God wants, what Jesus wants. I suppose you could say that maybe He wants us all to go that little way further and take the commitment, but that is for you to decide. This is in a way, a part of the facing up to life, but as a Christian follower of God. The choice is always ours because of our own free will that He gave to us.

A final bit to this chapter is about "Church", those whom we've met through attending Church and being a member of that family of God. There are those who are wonderful people who sustain us and keep that wonderful friendship "ticking over". I have I regret to say, had some problems with "loving" all those at Church though. In a couple of cases I went out of my way to "like" them, and in fact it was quite a task initially to even be civil to them such was my prejudice. After a while I was really depressed with myself, because I felt that I hadn't tried hard enough and why did I dislike these folks anyway?

The odd thing is that I stopped trying and started loving and found that all my prejudices were disappearing! That said, there will always be those who will be difficult to love, to like even, as some seem to relish being different and making their presence known by their ways. Sometimes it's just better to accept the fact that you're never going to reach them, you're never going to be able to be their friend. But I've learned that's OK, love them and keep the thoughts and prayers for them and then leave it to Jesus, and them!

I had an experience with a Christian friend who made me very sad and unable to be myself as this person wanted huge changes in me. I suspect the changes he desired have taken place gently and over time, maybe some of me hasn't, but the best way is to pray and to love them and God will do the rest, it's often the only way. Expectations can be a strange thing, they can stifle, they can inhibit, they can destroy. So be careful what you expect of God too, we don't have the answers or the formula, only He does, so prayers and listening is often the only way.

So if you have a friend, or someone that you feel is close, remember what God made us from.

My Friend

I had a friend who I thought cared,
that for my body and soul they shared;
But I was wrong and did not know,
just how the friendship we had would go.

It starts as mutual regard each for the other,
then as knowledge grows we both will smother,
all the wonderful things we found;
The help the love we nearly drowned.

Why do we see the best in each,
and then uncover and try to teach,
another way to see the Lord
but somehow really, there's no accord.

The Love the hate the fear of him
does nothing really, it seems a whim.
But as the time moves slowly on
the human part it dies, and is soon gone

A lesson here is what we learn
although the Christian love we yearn,
be careful how you treat your friend
it may just hurt them at the end.

Feb 2002

Chapter Four
What Do we want, what does He want?

When I started this book, I thought of merely putting in the poems and putting a bit of narrative between each one, a sort of explanation of what was behind the poem and what drove me to do it. But I felt that was not what was needed and wouldn't really do justice to what I was trying to do. I know that I've said earlier in the book, who's going to read it anyway, but somehow I felt that it needed to be more than just a book of poems. I was also quite scared to attempt to write a lot of the things that I have in this book, but why should I? it is true and it reflects the depth of my feelings and it shows how I questioned and wondered about the path that I feel is ahead.

After I came back to Church, which as I mentioned earlier was really as a result of my Dads death, I started confirmation classes and then about 18 months later I went on a "Cursillo" weekend as I explained in Chapter one. It's quite significant that both of these were to an extent as a result of meeting one of our most dear friends Jane Atkins whose name will appear many times in this book. The fact is that Jane was the "Lay Rector" or leader of the Cursillo weekend that Gen and I attended.

The problem with these weekends is that Cursillo lights a fire and you "want to do things", change things, give folks this "stuff" you receive. All the wonderful love received from wonderful people from all across the UK and in fact further a field too. You see this is how Cursillo works, prayers are offered from Christians from all over the country for the participants, but in reality this is a formula that is there for all to use, and for all our brothers and sisters.

These weekends act as a bit of a catalyst, some people get similar "awakenings" in other ways, but this overwhelming desire to do "something" is often great, but in fairness it needs channelling and it needs a bit of understanding from the one who's just returned or received this "awakening". I thought that God was calling me to do heaps of things, so I blundered blindly on doing "good" things. The problem is that I work full time, and was miles from home too (about an hour each way depending on traffic) I'm also getting older and not so capable of doing what I did say 10 years ago, I seemed to say yes to all the voluntary things that came along, and I started to grind to a halt. I became frustrated, depressed even hopeless in a way.

Have you ever wanted to go out and change the world? Help people to understand God, love Jesus, make the world a better place? Get steamed up because most people don't give a fig about God until tragedy strikes. (even then some still don't bother) Well this was me at that time, but I started to wonder what on earth did I want to do for Him, more importantly, what did He want me to do? I started to realise all the things I do were not naturally suited to me, I'd become a local councillor in 1995 and this had taken up loads of my personal time, but it's not naturally something I would or could do, I wanted to do loads more for the Church (again, something that I'd not been naturally doing), I was heavily into a local community group (another line of working unfamiliar to me) and as a result I got bogged down depressed forgetting my family, friends and most importantly, my wife.

What on earth was I meant to be doing? I found eventually I couldn't find the time to go to Church and I didn't meet with other Christians, I really thought I could do this on my own and that's not possible, we need each other to be able to do what Gods got in mind for us, but we also have to "de-clutter" our lives to do what He wants of us.

This long journey to and from work when I was away at Rugeley was a bit of a novelty for a start, I prayed on the way, and on the way back, but in the dark winter months it got tough and I felt I was doing nothing and why was I having to work all this distance away from home, preventing me from doing His will! I tried to understand what was the point in all of this and then I found that I had a lot of inspiration and I wrote some poems – here's one from a January morning!

Mists

Like life itself the mists show all,
we strain to see what's there and all;
The eye sees not, the ear can't hear,
each step, each tread, we dread, we fear.

The life we have the life we share;
Can you let go and show you care?
Does life scare you, do your mists lie low?
Along the tracks beyond your reach that go.

What lies beneath these thoughts inspire;
Does life burn like a funeral pyre.
Have you stopped dead and thought of life,
beyond the mask, the front, your strife?

I hurt inside the life endures,
In the world of fears there are no cures;
My pain I search but answers none,
If when the end is nigh, am I just gone?

Raise hope try hard use the power within;
Life's hopeless frightened tasks begin.
Believe don't fret don't feel beyond,
see life in ripples across some misty pond.

Beyond these mists your heart is this;
Where there's no pain no stress just bliss.
No matter where you seem to drown,
the mists will part as you see his crown.

14th January 2002

Note: Written after a drive to work on a very misty morning very ethereal and mysterious, thought provoking and so the thoughts of the morning I expected were lost and these words didn't come easily but they are recorded now for good or otherwise. I was feeling very depressed and was too, until putting these words together in the office at work.

That poem in a way, was really trying to make some sense of purpose for what I was doing. I prayed and prayed and nothing seemed to work. I'd worked in the defence industry for 28 years before being made redundant in 1999, so getting a job in anything other than that business seemed remote, hence this trek to and from Staffordshire, around 70 miles round trip each day. I felt sorry for myself and depressed about why I couldn't get a different job that would allow me to be closer to home where I could do all the things that I wanted to do for God. I tried very hard to get a job doing other things but although I got interviews I just couldn't land that job.

Maybe I too was a bit scared as to whether I could do it anyway, so perhaps I didn't try hard enough? Who knows?

Maybe, also I hadn't thought that possibly God had something in mind, and He might know what and when was the right time.

You see there was another factor and that was that I developed anxiety panic attacks around agoraphobia about 6 or 7 years ago and that has been very debilitating. Driving on motorways and in some terrains cause panic attacks and therefore travel has become a major difficulty. So what on earth was I supposed to do? I was working miles from home, which takes up loads of my time, I have this councillor role, which absorbs loads of time, and just to add a bit of interest to it all, I have agoraphobia, with panic attacks. Isn't that just fine, and I ask God what's this all about? How can I serve you Lord with all this conspiring against me. Well I can stop whingeing for a start. I can look to all the Christians who support and love me, and I can pray for help from God.

My agoraphobia has made me realise some things too, how hurt and damaged people can be, unseen! A broken leg is fairly obvious too, but the problems of anxiety are not quite so obvious and we don't tend to share these problems too often do we? It's a bit too close to home to talk about them.

But it does focus your mind about doing things for God. You see it's not the huge jobs he's after doing, even the so called menial jobs which we think have no impact, they all add up to the sum of what He wants. As long as one Christian makes a cup of tea to drink for those who thirst, we're actually giving something and that act as menial and insignificant, could be a turning point for that someone.

You may never know, you don't need to know – as long as that act is instrumental in making the difference for some one.

I think it's time for a poem again:-

The Journey

Leaves are falling, hearts are sprawling, can you see what happens here?
Unsure visions what you are, hearts that know not what you are.
Fear is what is deep inside, but what has caused this fire within?

See beyond above the glaring wrong or is it so and was it you?

Contentment could be what you really feel, be comfortable with you and you
and you.
Where is all this going to and from?

Do you see and can you see, would you know and could you speak?
Tell all that hear of what you know, the one's with hearing will be first to see
the path that's laid outspread, the way the sight the real within.

Did you ever feel so much so real, could you ever know what was laid before
you even then?

The way, the route the everlasting part that succours every soul that hears and
sees for real.

Where we've been is passed and learned but where we're going is just beyond the
understanding of our consciousness right here.

Let the everlasting glow and light of lights, transport the essence that is you, to
everlasting journey's end.

28th January 2003

Having ploughed through all that lot and considered great folks like Mother Theresa of Calcutta, I did have a bit of guilt about how she and others like her have done so much. But we are not all Mother Theresa's, we are who we are and what we are, and God's purpose is not always obvious. Also the time of life, or the trigger for when you start is not obvious or clear either.

I was 47 before I was confirmed, a bit late in life I thought, but I believe that was meant to be. I guess my maturity in spirit was taking place and the time became right, but I was so sure that I should go for ordination, without the slightest idea what that actually involved or meant. You see I hadn't listened or taken notice at all, just jumped in with both feet without consulting God, or anyone else, trying to do it on my own.

I mentioned earlier about this friend of ours, Jane Atkins, well she had already trod this path and must at times (and still must) have been amused at my thrashings about and some of the things I came up with. Mostly unfeasible, but what I wanted desperately to do and to achieve, but without prayer, and without real consideration of where I was and what I was doing. Jane in fact is now a Reverend, at present working in Norfolk after much trial and tribulations in getting a 'paid' job in the Church, and works very hard, harder than she should but she has such devotion and also has my thrashings to consider and put up with. This is the real test of my Christian friendship, someone who is a friend and listens as a Christian and still remains a friend! I must be blessed!

Again time for a poem and one that harps back to the child, the adolescent, the man learning and yearning:-

My Life

My life my yearning on this everlasting journey, as the child and as the
youth and where are we all going?

Dreaming with a mind that wanders, loves all with a love so tender, why
world do we struggle over you?

Our world so full of tenderness and warmth, coldness in the south and
north, what is our purpose here just now?

Gladly as my life unfolds I trade the years and watch my face as change I
must, but how is the purpose acted out?

I ask myself I pray aloud what are we now just throngs or crowds? And so I
sing my song of love for all ,

I'm dreaming with my mind that wanders loves all with a love so tender,
why world do we struggle over you?

Tell me of the days we spend together and those we are apart, tell me of the
yearning wished that we could both restart;

I listen now as rain is falling gentleness the rain is falling soothing all the
land and me as well;

Tell me stories of the heart and love and why we all should be lovers of the
world and of each other,

So why am I still seeking looking searching in my heart, maybe the purpose
is just here!

3rd May 2004

Funnily enough I'm on holiday as I write this part of the book. We're in a place that's quite nice, but predominately full of the elderly and infirm. I'd failed to realise how intolerant we get as we get older. This may seem unjust and rather selfish in my comments, but it's true, there's some really difficult people among these older lot, maybe I'm one of them in reality. Once again it's all down to tolerance and expectations, because of the advanced years and the fact that some are incapacitated, there becomes an expectation that their need is now greater somehow. Elderly people do suffer indignity and are abused, but so are children and young people.

We all take part and we all suffer at the hands of those who cannot, or will not understand and fail to compromise in life situations. Jesus had this amazing ability to look for and find ways and means of reaching people. I looked at a bunch of people here (not excluding me either!) and thought now then, if you put a bunch of new age travellers in amongst them what would you see then? Or, how about a load of asylum seekers? Well it's unfair as we're in a rather expensive holiday venue, but if they'd paid their bit and arrived, how welcome would they be? I suspect not very. But you see Jesus mingled with and talked to all sorts, not something we all can do successfully and from this we would understand something and that is, he's not actually expecting that from us all, but what he is expecting is tolerance and trying to make contact and be Christian people, to all God's creations. A tall order I know, but worthy of what he sacrificed for us.

I guess that this is something that I still struggle with, God, whose only son was allowed to be vilified, judged by those who were jealous and fearful of him and then put to death in a way that is all too hard to imagine. I would imagine that many of those who selfishly push themselves in front and grasp at everything as their years decline don't have the slightest thought about God's huge sacrifice for us through his only son. It makes you feel like rushing up to them and shouting out what selfish old so and so's you all are! But what would that achieve, apart from getting all their backs up, you'd be another religious crank not a good Christian doing God's work, you're expected to be meek and mild and take the slap on the other cheek, well it's ok in theory but just you try it some day.

Poem time:-

Look Inside

Did you ever look at your face and really look inside?
Did you see a wave, the source, the inward tide?
Was the face perfect without lines, without a single mark?
Or did you notice a greying even blackening something almost dark?

Did you look into the eyes so deep and see what's really there?
Or did you see nothing more than the return of a distant stare?
How far did you look though, past the earthly you
Could you see something more, towards a different view?

The soul you can see through the eyes of a man
I've heard it said many times and I think you can.
But what lurks within, what is it we hide
When once you are soul bared and then opened wide.

Do you use your eyes to see as a human can see,
Or can you adjust for a moment and look clear as He?
For the world and it's mysteries and the promise beyond
Are part of His message His Loving so fond.

But as usual we cloud over the eyes with a mist
Forgetting our viewing our existence is already kissed,
By the One who rules over the world that we know
We still seem unable His wonders to show.

23rd December 2001

Here's a thought to consider for a moment or two, have you ever crept into a nice quiet little corner and thought great, away from all the hustle and bustle of life, no kids, screaming or yelling, no miserable old so & so's whingeing, nothing but peace and quiet, no cars, no lorries, nothing – at peace completely, wonderful! Well now what! After about 15 minutes you'd get up and start to wonder, some probably would have gone barking mad by now, but the quest for peace is not just the inert sterile quiet room, it is far more that that, but what is it really and how to achieve it, what is God's plan for that and for us?

My way was to say "Yes" to everything, "I'll do it" and then what? Get bogged down and achieve nothing, splitting up into loads of bits doing no one thing well. Does this sound familiar? Or anything like you? Or are you one of these wonderfully disciplined folks who can say No and can be in charge and do what needs to be done. Well if you are, let me know how you do it coz I'm hopeless!

I need to be amongst Christians who constantly keep me thinking about doing the sensible thing and praying for guidance to ensure I'm a bit more structured and focused in what I'm doing and need to be doing. I often say how much I like people, I like chatting to them, with them, and sharing our lives and experiences, and sometimes touching on the "tough bits". How many people can you do that with though? I'd guess not that many, but we do need to be able to talk, relate whatever, especially sometimes when we find the going rough.
But trusting in that person is always going to be hard too, for the world has, regrettably those who will listen and then abuse that trust.
The Christian way is for fellowship groups within our Churches – committed to each other to share that path, that route, that difficult route to Christ, for He said that being a Christian would not be easy and we all know that I'm sure.

Here's a poem to help that:

Walking

Walked upon the shore line kicking up the sand;
Meandered here and there, aimless nothing planned;
And yet somehow a purpose always in my mind;
The way I'd walked towards the land I really wasn't blind.

The sun was shining on the waves, little white tops leapt;
The sand between my toes was warm as further on I crept;
Disturbed a sea bird on my way who fluttered noisily aloft;
And yet his protest calls soon mingled with the rhythmic waves so soft;

My progress slow across the sand I felt for just a moment lost;
And yet I knew that I was not, like driftwood that was tossed;
You've seen those weathered timbers on shores and coasts abound;
A kind of life's reminder of travellers resting, who never make a sound.

Alone I clambered up the dunes towards that kindly light;
It was twinkling through the trees just there, it was a welcome sight;
I tried to think of who was there to greet my journey's end;
A little message on the wind I wish that they would send.

And so on trust I journey on towards this distant light;
It fills my eyes it fuels my soul, I journey day and night;
My hand is in the hand of all who tread this hallowed way;
It seemed a moment then I felt another's hand while striding on my way.

That distant light so far away it seemed was closer now by far;
I looked around and saw a host, the light now like a star;
I saw the faces near to me all glowing from that starry hue;
I glimpsed among the throng again and saw that face I knew.

29th August 2003

We talk of what we want, or what He wants of us, this chapter in fact is about that, so I ask a question of you as I did of me ages ago and in fact still do. "What am I doing here and what do I want to do?" At school I was not a brilliant scholar, I excelled at things that I was interested in and other things, well you know! As I approached the time I would leave full time education and go out to work, I really didn't know what to do. All I did know was I had to get a job to earn a living.

At this time God's purpose for me was the least of my concerns, and yet, somehow there was a constant wondering about life and what was in the future. I slipped between jobs and worked for a frozen food company for a while, who sent me to Nottingham on a training course. It was a bit daunting initially, I had no transport, couldn't drive, so I went there on the train which was quite fun really (I was about 17 or 18 at the time). Then staying in a hotel near to a large Arboretum was novel, the bus trips into the works were quite an adventure for me too. Nights were a bit odd though, as I found making friends difficult, male or female but I did eventually find some friends, and the nights were quite different then. I had my first taste of city life, seeing prostitutes at work, met some transvestites one night. I had my first real meeting with homosexuals or Gays as we prefer to say now, West Indians and other ethnic folks a whole new slice of life I'd never encountered before. To say that I was overawed is an understatement, as a 17 year old from a little town, boy was I naïve and the world had some very real lessons for me to learn.

Funny thing is though that I had no real lead, no actual clear path as to where I wanted to go or where I needed to go. The chap I was there with was very streetwise and must have thought of me as a real pratt, I was completely overawed by it all – a kid in amongst his first taste of real life. Then one day I was a bit down, I actually contemplated my own mortality, I realised that I was going to die. I was actually coming back to the hotel I was staying in and walking past the arboretum, and the thoughts just filled my mind. I'd seen death on TV and films but of course actors re-appeared in the next film or show, there was no reality in this but all of a sudden along with all this new life, this alien way of life I found out in my own way that one day anytime in fact, I was going to die.

The blackness of it as I thought of what it meant, being no one, not existing, snuffed out finished. I was so melancholy I was shocked and unable to feel for days. I couldn't contemplate life because of the death I'd just envisaged. Just a funny part of those thoughts were that I hadn't yet had sex and I was most concerned at one point that I might just die a virgin!, what a waste! I expect that young people have all sorts of crisis as they grow up but my sudden encounter with big city life opened my eyes to a whole new part of life I just couldn't come to terms with and then before even getting old I found out even I would die one day. I talked to my mum about some of these things and she was a great support and I suppose her background of church in a small way did help me. I couldn't find a way to church though, it was all too formal and there was no one of my age to relate to. This is a big challenge as well today as how many young people might be interested but can't find anyone to relate to and help them to find a place with God in your Church?

So what's this got to do with what He wants and we want? Well in fact it's all about where we start and how life prepares us and God watches us as we mature, grow up or whatever. I spent the next 30 years moving into a job that I neither enjoyed or excelled at particularly, but never had the real guts to move out of until in 1999 I had to leave because I was forced to by redundancy. I still can't decide where to go and how to achieve it, but I pray for help and guidance and I do seem to be making some impact in my environment for God, even though I don't recognise it sometimes.

When I was searching out another job I found one quite unexpectedly, working to help people back to work, bit ironic in a way. I thought that it was the answer to a prayer and I was destined to be able to help and do Gods work through this. I was quite taken aback at how this initiative actually worked and I was able to see also the good and bad things about unemployment, what it does to people and what some people do to others as a result of it.

I mentioned earlier that I met a Christian work colleague through this new job who was a very devout Christian and had huge expectations I believe, of me. I was going through a very bad time when all of this occurred, I was suffering from extreme agoraphobia and anxiety panic attacks whilst desperately trying to make the job work, it was the time too when I was Mayor of my home town. I had many problems and I tried to do this, take it all on, on my own. I couldn't find time to meet with other Christians for fellowship and prayer so I tried to be big enough to do it all on my own, a recipe for disaster and that's pretty well what occurred.

My colleague discovered my weaknesses and "Achilles heel" and reckoned that I was unworthy to do the job and lead as I was attempting to do. I thought that I had been hearing God and following where He was calling and maybe this was a lesson, or a time of learning for me as the situation soon became untenable. I left the job and went back into the defence industry but I did however move on and started to attend an ECLF course (Exploring Christian

Life and Faith) and I started a steady Church attendance helped as usual by our good friend Jane Atkins.

I started to resolve to a small extent, my agoraphobia problems, but more importantly I returned to Church and taking Eucharist with Christian people, people who have become very dear to Genesta and myself, so is there a purpose in all of this, I wonder?

Here's another poem:

Can I see?

All and everything that life gives over now,
The giving, taking, sharing; my life for what it's worth and how?.
Stepping forward into light, shrinking back when dark is nigh;
Was it all because of what was done? That heaving heavy sigh?
The act undone, not done, forgotten; was the guilt so real?
Or was it merely human frailty, the mortal sin we have and feel?
It always has and always will, be in your nature, your human kind, your
way,
And who is there? Who is so fit to say and damn your way, the act, what
did you say?

Or was it not so much what did you do or say or not?, that broke the heart
the fragile soul?.
Where in the world, where in the heavens, where is the torment solved,
where are you whole?
Sit within Gethsemane with me; let us feel and have the sorrow, fear His
final confrontation plea,
The knowledge of the Son Divine who's future, condemned by others,
done, not done, said not said, can I now see?

20th December 2002

I suppose I'll end this chapter by saying this much, don't push too hard for that "what do I want, or what does He want" Some may find the direction and be moved very fervently very quickly, but most I think, the lesser mortals among us will wander and struggle, but one thing I have learned by the mistakes and advice I've received is this, give it to Jesus, He will direct you and help. It may seem hard at times, it may seem as if nothing is actually happening and you are doing nothing, but only He knows the truth and what is right for you. There are those who can help, advise, pray with you, but trust in the Spirit, on the Lord when doing so, for there may be those who expect of you more than you should or can give. They do not know you or your capabilities like Jesus does. Only Christ can and does, so trust in Him, be conscious of your Christian brothers and sisters but remember they too are human and are as fallible as you and I, our only true and loving lead can come from He who knew us before we were what we are, trust in the Lord God almighty.

The next poem is a thought on the way I saw our lives in context of the striving we do and what we just need to stand back occasionally and see the world and it's immensity in perspective.

Dust

Dust just here, blowing by my naked feet,
Across the ground and down the concrete street
What was in that dust I saw just then?
It crosses through my mind just now and again.

I look across the void of city life
The place humanity now lives out in strife;
Blocks of stone and concrete stare at me
Hard reality civilisation, what do I see?

I look at dust as in the city street it plays
Moving always, in one place it never stays;
Where to next where from it came?
The question always in my mind the same.

I stride upon the concrete floor of city street
I walk amongst the city folks who do I meet?
Rushing here and rushing there,
Never see the dust accumulating, where?

The man just there, so big and healthy has no care
Eats his fast food meal and tosses off the paper, does he share?
Throws the last few crumbs away without a thought
And so those crumbs as dust become but nought.

The girl who's standing over there so beautiful and slim,
Takes the jacket off her shoulders tosses it away, a whim
And in the rubbish it rots away and joins the dust
Did that matter, untrendy, totally un-fussed.

The wind blows over all the buildings tall
And dust swirls endlessley across the city sprawl
The wind it blew some in my eye
I peered through tears it caused, into the clear blue sky.

Every speck of dust a life in all eternity will blow
Every tear it causes shed because the life did go.
Every grain, each and every speck of dust that moves
A promise of forever through its movement proves.

25th November 2003

Chapter Five
Relationships?

I got hold of a book by Phillip Yancey (Yes another one! In fact I reckon he'll be asking for royalties at this rate!) called "Reaching for the Invisible God". I was interested in this because I'd had difficulties with relationships as a kid and now I was contemplating this relationship with God, some being, I neither seem to be able to speak to, touch, hear or see. So how do you have that relationship?

My dad and I had a strange relationship, I think we were pretty much distant in our ways and thoughts, but we never really talked so how could I make that assumption anyway? My granddad died when I was only 10 but I'd liked him although he was a bit of a grumpy old man, but my dad apparently hated him and this was mutual because when the old boy died he left a message that none of the family should go to the graveside so to speak. I was much troubled by that but that was his wish.

School was difficult too, although I attended a mixed infants school which was as far as I can recall, OK. The next one was a boys only and it was pretty tough, some of the towns "more interesting" characters attended that one and if you were "sensitive" or "shy" or slightly moved to the "less aggressive" you were sure to be bullied or at the very least "pushed around" a bit.
A common enough scenario I guess, but having an "interesting" home life too isn't that uncommon either so many of you may well know a deal about what I'm saying.

My dad was not a Christian, at least he never admitted to it whilst I was about, and the local Church was hardly one that you'd be seen in, well not at my age anyway. So the opportunity to be involved with or in Christian life was never something that I was likely to get drawn into. Yet I did derive some instruction from school R.E. classes and strangely enough a "comic" publication I used to get did cover the life and passion of Jesus. The final part His crucifixion, left me with a very deep emotional scar, one that was to cause many future problems in my relationship with God.

Going back to my comments about school days, the RE Teacher used to say that the Bible was "a book of civilisation", rules to live your life by and for a number of years I sort of understood that and felt pretty happy with those comments. It sort of gave me a "handbook for life" scenario which I could feel had answers to solve the problems I would encounter as I got older. I met my wife whilst very young, we were in our late teens. I wanted to be married more so than Gen initially and again I was not really thinking through what marriage was actually all about. Luckily I married the right girl for although our courtship at times was a bit stormy, we paved the way for a strong marriage. The fact is that the first marriage to come apart, that certainly I saw, was that of a good friend of us both. His wife had been difficult in their courting days (look at that old fashioned word "courting", but we did it!!) and also demanded a lot as they approached marriage.
I hadn't known much about their relationship early on save for some of the things that upset and hurt our friend, the fact is he was very wounded on a number of times.

Somehow, after they were married we seemed to drift apart, I saw him with other girls and he was pretty open about it too. Their marriage was blessed with kids eventually and I supposed that this would help and he'd spend more time at home. The reverse was the case and suddenly I felt stuck in the middle (and Gen too) with two people who were now on a collision course. I felt duty bound to support my mate, but it was not easy as I felt in a way, he was wrong because of his philandering. I also seemed to envy his ability to attract these girls which I found a great issue due to my background of inability to form friendships with any ease. I then tried to understand the breakdown of communications as it started to happen. There is nothing more devastating is there, than watching the whole thing go wrong, but if you step in to help, boy you're in a lot of trouble, or can be.

I watched as did Gen, umpteen marriages go wrong and we learned many lessons about human nature and when people feel wronged and hurt. Gen's family had one which was particularly messy and finished up with family at opposing ends of the world literally. After all these tragic endings I was drawn to write words in defence of one rather than the other so to speak, but it's actually trying to face the fact that one has made it happen as it did, but what was it that broke the marriage, the relationship entirely as it did?

Here are those words:

What did You do?

Your want your need your lust for him,
The blindness of your want without a thought for anyone but you.
Did you think of anyone but you ,your whim?
And now through all the years that passed can you perceive the selfishness
of you?

What did you want why did you take?
And now you've had him all and then discarded for another?
How did you feel and when the heart did break,
Was the blindness all complete and still complete even with this other?

And now you look at life before,
The life you made come true for you and what for him now left behind?
The fractured fragments of what, the score?
And did you ever contemplate at all the years, were you ever kind?

Satisfy the self, the wanton yearn,
Why should I not take it all, it's mine this world to grab not share!
But of the pain inflicted did you learn?
The damage to his life and what of her and others, did you care?

And still you grasp at worldly gift!
Your eyes are sealed the ears tight shut but does your soul receive?
What does it take your heart to shift?
When will you rest, what of your foolish desires of hope as you yourself
deceive.

Read the words can you see what's meant,
If only you could see the hardship, the waste of life, bequest.
Only when your life you've spent,
Will the final stages of the realising of the waste, the ultimate final selfish
test.

16th February 2004

Sometimes it's easy to take sides and to be "one sided", easy to dislike one or the other party or partner for as many reasons as there are questions as to why the marriage or relationship failed. Being able to forgive or love the other party to the injured one that takes a lot but it's what we should do and how Jesus would expect us to be.

I sometimes wonder how you'd talk about issues like this with Jesus sitting there in the room, would we be quite so sure about whose fault caused the problem in the first place? I wonder about how I'd be, knowing He was sitting there, but actually that's what it amounts to, He is there all the time so what does that make our discussions like. Have you ever thought of it that way? I did and it's made me think a lot more about the sort of things I say and how I put together my arguments, but we ought to be natural in what we say all the time, but as humans, invariably many factors modify or have a bearing on what we do, say or imply. But God knows that and forgives in a way we don't and can't understand, but this is part of the relationship that is very special and only capable between you and me and God.

There's that famous part of the Bible read at weddings about Love. 1 Corinthians 13: 4 – 13.
"Love is patient, love is kind. It does not envy, it does not boast, it is not proud. It is not rude, it is not self-seeking, it is not easily angered, it keeps no record of wrongs. Love does not delight in evil but rejoices with the truth. It always protects, always trusts, always hopes, always perseveres".

A friend of ours, and I'm sure many have also used this suggestion, said "replace your name for "Love" and see how it goes.

I think I could fare reasonably well to a point and with those who are easy to love, but could I do it for all, irrespective of who they are and what they are and see how the score is then, I know, I fail badly!

One of my greatest friends parted from his wife recently and I haven't seen him or her for ages. The odd thing is this is a man whom I have great personal respect for and who worked tirelessly for young people for a number of years, kids who were from very difficult backgrounds. He was understanding and very capable with them. But who knows what causes the breakdown in a relationship? I pray for all who have difficult relationships, but this comes back to the relationship with God, for as I said earlier on how do we actually make that relationship work?

Ours breakdown for various reasons, try writing down what has caused a fall out with friends relatives, anyone you have had a falling out with. But then think about Jesus, about God. I spent some time in my previous book mentioning about my difficulty with God over my mothers death from cancer. Also how I tried to "make it" on my own, leaving God on one side, thinking that by being insular, but asking Him as a Father to help and sustain me. Again it's crawling into a corner and being shut off from the "hard prickly" world, it is not what it's all about no matter how tempted we are to go for that option.

Think of someone you really love and trust, what is it about them that gives you this loving feeling, this trust, this comfort of being with them. Why should this be more so with this person than anyone else you can think of. God has no pre-conditions such as we make, He only asks for love, supreme love that lasts forever and is all embracing. You see, next to my wife this person to me was mum. OK you argue the sense the reasons and the whys and wherefores of that but I could talk to her without condition without reservation, totally open. But when she died all of that was lost, except that there are times when I ask for her help her comments her trust. However, as you know there is no way she can respond, not in the human physical way as once we did. I know she is with God and she, along with many many others are with the spirit as Jesus promised us. When I ask for help and I talk now, it is to Jesus, just like He's over there. I felt it was a pretty one sided affair for a time and still have my doubts, but the discussions are more prayers than maybe I realise, or ever realised and maybe this is what He's always wanted from a relationship such as we His children can offer.

He listens when I'm broken, shattered, happy, joyous and He takes me when I'm horrible and bad tempered, unconditionally – what a relationship; only that a King of all Creation could give.

As A Child

With the eyes of a child I once saw you there,
I knew although so small, that you would always care.
I didn't understand what adults meant when they would talk aloud,
I didn't know at all their speech it was really in a cloud.
They talked and swore and said "You'll never understand"
And if I answered back they'd sometimes laugh, but often use a hand.

With the eyes of a child I once saw you there,
I cannot even try to think of how I saw you, even if I stare.
My world was so much clearer then and so were you my Lord.
I didn't even have to try too hard to understand your word.
Your voice it sprang from Bible text and I could never fault
Your word was right your actions clear and never need to halt.

I looked with eyes that saw no wrong and wanted to know more,
And as I grew I thought so much and really felt quite sure.
I stared so hard at clouds up there which covered up your view;
I really didn't need to worry then, I always felt you knew.
I want to have my heart returned the one I had just then,
To feel so close to you and know that childish love again.

The child who then knew Jesus, who is our lifelong friend,
He will always take you back again and all His love will send.
I am that child he stands still now,
And to your greatness, loving, caring spirit bow,
Forgive me Lord as by my bed I kneel and start to pray,
As was I then a child to you, I am your child today.

23rd November 2002

A continuing relationship needs to have input, watering the flowers so to speak, and what can we do about that? I find that as I get older I find the way we live increasingly difficult, people and the way they are in life because they do not want to have these relationships, maybe they crave them too much and mess up in the process, who knows but the delicate balance of what we are and what we aspire to be can sometimes be the undoing of the purpose of our existence, our relationship with the world.

I talked of the relationship with my dad earlier on and how I found him a difficult person to have a relationship with, as father and son. As a person I would probably have walked away and thought too difficult and left him to stew in his own juices. How many are there in the world like that?

And how many do we not even try to understand why they are as they are? Later revelations about dad drew me to believe that he was a man in torment, a man driven by his own demons but unable to make that relationship that he craved, the meaningful one that would satisfy his soul and make his existence on earth fulfilling and easier to bear, not only for him but for the people whom he knew. As his son I could never believe the way that he went about things, the child saw the thing so simply and he could not see the basic simplicity in the child perspective, but then that's true of us all, especially when we try to do the same thing from our advancing years and with the baggage we have amassed over the years getting to where we are right now.

Christian relationships are also funny things, trying to establish the reality of the person who you get to know and think well if the will of God is in them they are perfect ones to make a relationship with. Not always so, as we tend to think that our relationship with God is the right one, forgetting that the real one making the relationship is Jesus, and that we are the sinful children that he calls to do His work, but recognises that we are after all, only human. So what of this Christian relationship? Well it is really down to the fact that although we are Christians and we love Jesus and we all love God, we don't necessarily have the ability to give to love and to accept that we all see that relationship from slightly different angles. I know that we must see the words of the Bible as the words passed to us by the prophets and by Jesus Himself, we must see our own failings in understanding what is said, what was meant and what we are called to do.

The next poem I wrote ages ago (well it feels like it now) and was another "child's eye" view of things but it had the undertones in it of the relationship theme that I was desperately trying to embrace. I said that I had difficulty trying to form friendships, youngster relationships, but was not very able to do this. I felt hurt and I suppose I still do, so there were times when I used to "put up the barriers", keeping the world out, stopping the pain by making sure no one could know me fully and therefore get in and hurt me. The problem is that this does nothing for the relationships does it? How can you have this relationship where there's no interaction, no honesty no understanding, just a sterile inert set of pleasantries designed to make sure that we can communicate with each other. Can we deal with our God like that? Insulate yourself from Him and pretend that we can manage without Him and tell Him only what is deemed OK by you and me, or me primarily and that which causes me the least amount of hurt, when in reality He knows only too well what is really going on, inside around and within, so here's the next poem, another around the "child" but it seems to be right for the subject we're dealing with:

A Child

The fields were green and life so fine
the world and all its wonders they were mine.
I was a child and with those childlike eyes
I never thought of any heartfelt sighs.

I knew no fear, except of men who often frightened me;
A child can sense the evil there, their eyes can really see.
But when you're young you have no way to know if this is right or wrong,
You carry on your little life and hum your little song.

You grow up knowing little more than what is meted out,
Does it matter if it is a fist that falls, or just a heavy shout.
You look for solace in yourself away amongst the stars,
Staring into who knows where, you live for hours and hours.

But when reality stares at you, and grow up as you surely will;
You find that world is not the norm a very bitter pill.
The child that once knew nothing more than peace within a field,
must suddenly find what manhood gives and to the world must yield.

The need to have the love, the care and have your dreams to share,
Your heart will break, the world would fall if only you could dare.
The journey from the child to man is not so many years;
And down the path you walk alone you pick up all those awful fears.

It's then the need to know the man who saved us with his life;
Will comfort share and love your dreams and take away your strife.
He took the pain the agony on that cross, and never ever complained at all,
And you have suffered silent all those years but he would comfort you,
you'll never fall.

Why then as I look back in anguish at those lost days of youth and child,
Will I stand fast and hear the words from him so very very mild.
It is because the child can only live if for the moment given by the King
You are his child and to His feet your soul you'll ever bring.

Fear not the world and all its sinful men, who'd take away your childish
days;
They may ruin this life and make you hate with bitterness that cries and
stays.
All who suffer in the world trust in the Lord and all his goodness He'll give
to you,
Just trust in Him and Love His will that's all you really have to do.

5th October 2002

We often formulate some strong relationships where we work I certainly did, I worked in Leicester at Marconi Radar Systems for 27 years starting there when I was 24 years of age and leaving through redundancy at 51. A life time really in one firm so not only did I see a lot come and go, but eventually a number of people became significant in my life although no one got beyond the "barriers" completely.

There were some who caused me much pain and I watched them also when they found life dishing out some very difficult times for them, it happens to us all even those that seem to be immune from being "damaged" too.

There was a man whom I knew there who was very difficult to like and to know, he contracted cancer of the throat and yet he continued to come to work bandaged over his throat almost until he died.

I could never forget his face, his trudging to work and the pain on his face as he carried on knowing I guess his fate. I still couldn't like him even though I felt for his pain, his indignity as he faced his final confrontation. Could I have been witnessing any other event without compassion? (could any of us?)

I befriended a Ugandan Asian chap (these were the people that were expelled from Uganda by the dictator Idi Amin in the 70's) during the years there, a nice bloke with a smashing family and we had many pleasant years working together, in fact through him I learned of the "caste" system amongst Indian culture, a bit of a shock when I started to understand the ways of their culture (something I knew nothing about at this time), a bit of a shock when I started to learn of their culture whilst working in the "big company" culture. This caused some upsets in the workplace and did nothing to help working relationships. It was also part of the difficulty I had and which grew in me about "class" systems and how we treat each other as "employers" and "employees". There were some "foremen" (probably better known as shop floor supervisors now) whom I found straight forward people who were fair and really honest, treating the workforce with dignity and honesty, but there were others who abused their position and strained relations even with the "better" ones.

I was lucky I had a boss who was a tough task master but a man of high morals and very honest and who treated us all well, even though he was pretty strict but we knew where we were with him, something you didn't with the others who would exploit you and use or abuse as they saw fit. And yet among all these people that I met and I was trying to come to terms with in my early years of working relationships, was a man who I met and never realised was a Christian and was later to meet through the Anglican Cursillo movement. A man whom I had liked and could quite easily, through him, have become a Christian sooner if I'd had the ability to trust and allow relationships to grow. But I was either not ready or maybe the Lord had other ideas, so 20 odd years later when I made my Cursillo at Launde Abbey in 1995 there was this man, Bob Davies welcoming my return to the Christian fellowship via the Anglican Cursillo movement. Bob had been a buyer at Marconi for years and someone that I knew, just like many others but never allowed him in, just like the dozens of others I got to know through all those many years, but never allowed in either.

Another poem, and this time one that asks why was Jesus crucified for us and to see that we know what he did for us and help us to make sense of our senseless world.

Why?

Why were you crucified my Lord?
What was it really for?
They tell me it was all for sin, and saving souls like me.

You came amongst us made some friends
And how did they respond?
There's one who caused the pain to You, he lives in name for all.

Come back and see us, love us now;
Be with us all for ever more,
Seal our fates with Love You give, make whole this world once more.

2nd May 2005

Just to finish this chapter, the test of relationships is the way that we deal with each other, you see, that I just mentioned about my friend Bob Davies, a man that I knew years ago and now I know him and his wife as Christian brothers and sisters, someone that I know will be for me forever, how can I fault that? Also, through the Cursillo movement I have made many Christian friends that pray for me and are always glad to see me, even if I've been forgetful, off hand, or what ever, prepared to forgive my human failings just like Jesus asked of us. How many others have I not recognised because I was unable to let them in when I should have been capable of doing and being the person that I need to be, God will be the judge of that and hopefully the work that we do as we become the makers of real relationships we may be able to say with conviction "His will be done."

Chapter: Six
I Have a Dream:

I was looking at Martin Luther King's speech recently, well listening actually, "I have a dream" and then looked at the problems we're having throughout the world. Iraq, Bosnia, Africa etc etc etc. It seems there needs to be a dream for all of this and all these folks. I've had dreams about people being this or that and how we'd all sit together whatever we are, religious conviction wise or colour, creed or anything else that separates us for that matter.

A while ago, Genesta and I went to a place called "Fox Hangers" near Devizes and it was a wonderful place near to the canals (The Kennet & Avon) which we dearly love, and there I wrote some poetry. It was me dreaming again. I'm good at that, not much else but that is a speciality of mine!, so this is why that dream of Martin Luther King's about "Little white and black kids" always struck home with me because I feel the goodness around and why should it be reserved for the few, even in dreams.

Poems from Devizes:

Life's Belief?

Of all the things I've done that's passed,
All the friendships, comrades, memories now amassed.
Regrets are many, when you recall,
How many times you promised much, and didn't call.
The memory of many friends you knew,
and across the years you take the view;
The loves, the friends, the one's you hate;
Are all these things now left too late?.
Your life is touched by some who pass this way,

You want that moment for all time to stay,
But time moves on and we do too,
And with it changes to our earthly view.
Remember if you can that chap you met
The joy of being with them, the world was set.
Now twenty years have come and gone
Could you remember if that's the one?
The phases of your life in stark relief
Say much about you and your total life's belief.

Devizes 27th September 2002

And even more 'dreamy' again, I was looking above at the clouds the sky and all around us and started on the next poem, just about, of course, Clouds.

Clouds

High above the fields and vales,
Spreading right above those wholesome dales;
Masquerading as bits of drifting cotton wool
Coloured red and grey and oh so full.
Watch them cover over a blazing sun
And then the colours they'll start to run.

The shafts of light burst through the grey
Hurtle earthward and where'd they stray?
A little white one over there is lost and on his own;
It looks so lonely, tearful, all alone.
And then majestic in horizon deepening to black,
A grumbling storm cloud towers above the stack.

The sunlight disappears from view
And struggles vainly it's light to strew.
A little piece departs this brooding mass,
And to one side it twirls to pass.
A patter on the ground just there,
And from the heavens stare,

A gentle rain comes tumbling down
And lands so softly on your crown.
Watch them flee across the sky
Those clouds of thunder, rain or fluffy fly.
They make each day what it is for
A patchwork in the sky, adore!.

Again in Devizes - - 27th September 2002

I have one of those minds that has lots of good ideas, too many really and then want to see those ideas put into action, and that's where I'm hopeless. I couldn't organise that event in a brewery!, so I flit from this to that and get people all upset because I never seem to be able to see some things through. But that's how some of us are, how could you tolerate that but the world needs the dreamers, its "butterflies" the ones who are full of ideas but so poor at seeing them through. Having these dreams are fine but then there needs to be the strong ones who make these dreams happen. These are the ones who I have difficulty with, so what they think of me who knows!!! But its true, without all these go –getters the dreamers dream would stay just dreams – God intends all of these things and makes us how we are to make certain they are done. The problem is that we sometimes don't realise and understand the way we need, to home in on what we're good at and leave the "other stuff" to those who are good at it and recognise that.

We fall into the trap too often of misunderstanding the strength of others because we see them as failings – the fact is our strengths should be complimentary not in competition. Then seeking the right "language" to be understood, that can be a huge problem too, so much so that huge chasms can open up which should never exist at all. But we make them because we fail to recognise the strength in the ability that others have, even though they appear to lack what we want to see, the truth is they possess what we do not and acts to compliment what our abilities are, if only we put the jigsaw together huge amounts of good work, good things can happen, if we are capable of seeing that.

So that need to 'share', to know that we can rely on that someone to help with 'that' idea 'that' piece of life that's causing us 'that' bit of a problem, someone to be 'that' support which draws to the time for another poem:

Lean on Me

Share each moment of a life, a life we have for just a fleeting time, to learn,
to love, to hold each others hand:
Share the good times and the bad, each time we feel the way ahead too
tough:

Lean on Him, lean on me, lean on all who love the Lord.

Share with me the sorrow, Share with Him the sorrow, Cry a little on the
shoulder, any shoulder;
A shoulder that once had carried sin and pride; a shoulder bruised and
beaten.

Lean on Him, lean on me, lean on all who love the Lord.

Share at last the gladness, the love revealed, the sin forgiven, share His joy;
Share it with Him and share now with all who love the Lord; but most of
all;

Lean on Him, lean on me, lean on all who love the Lord.

Share with all the fondest love, the way we all have fears and fright;
Share the terror of your life, with Him, with me, share it now with all who
love the Lord.

Lean on Him, lean on me, lean on all who love the Lord.

Share the passing of the night, the passing of a life, saved and precious held
within the hands;
Hands pierced with nails of hate, pierced to show the love He gave, share
His honour and His grace.

Lean on Him, lean on me, lean on all who love the Lord.

Never feel that you're alone, share the peace that is with all, now and for all
time sharing with our saviour Lord.
Share His pain and share His shame, share with Him the path He strode
for whatever stands before you, blocks your way, your path, your walk to
Calvary.

Lean on Him, lean on me, lean on all who love the Lord.

Share with Him those final moments, as the sin the evil of the world died
too;
His resurrection was confirmed and with it the promise we would share His
glory, the magnificence of redemption

Lean on Him, lean on me, lean on all who love the Lord.

We have no fear when share with Him, we all shall share His mighty vic-
tory -- We share His kingdom for Eternity.
Share the Mighty majesty, for all you ask of Him is Jesus remember me
when you come into your Kingdom.

31st March 2004

Now then, have you a dream? What could it be, think about it very carefully, come on any dream: - winning the lottery? Winning "Who wants to be a millionaire" on TV, being a successful writer, painter or whatever. These may not be particularly good examples maybe but you go on anyway and think of that dream.

So what makes the dream so important to you anyway, what would it do if it became a reality? Some things are fairly obvious, if you won a lot of money what would you do with it? Some dreams are quite simple ones to us. I should imagine that someone who has just been bereaved would have very different dreams than someone who is sitting in a comfortable happy and homely relationship. Also If you're sitting in the middle of a desert in war torn Africa or some other trouble spot in the world, the content of your dreams would be very different. The fact is, they're just as important, each of these dreams as they reflect where we are at that time in our lives.

Real seasoned dreamers are odd folks, as they dream about all sorts of diverse things. I had dreams about winning loads of money so I could use it for good and worthy things, although there may have been a slight amount of selfishness in that, as of course I'd also be very financially stable too! Perish the thought!!

I continue to dream of wonderful communities that live in harmony and peace, I dream of places without strife and war, and then I turn the TV on and "bump", down to earth I drop. I still dream though, and I still want to help for Gods sake, but sometimes reality is a tough reminder that they are dreams, and making them into reality is the real test of anyone. Martin Luther King's words should never be discarded, he was a dreamer on a grand scale in a way, but with Gods help his dream was realised as America is a much better place than once it was for the black communities. The problem is that as one area of His work seems to be realised, another is always there, so keep the dreaming going!!

When I started this book I never thought that I'd be sitting in bed at midnight scribbling out bits of notes like this, but I never considered writing a full sized book either! I ought to be in bed dreaming other dreams and not burning the candle at both ends! But that's dreamers for you!

Anyway, you see, talking about dreams and then the TV in fact I needed to set down these notes due to a TV programme that was on this very night. It was in two parts this programme and it was about the pop group ABBA. I quite liked ABBA back in the 70's (I was heavily into Pink Floyd and other bands like that as a rule, but they were "catchy") I also had a bit of a fascination about one of the girls in the group too. (better watch out here, otherwise my wife will be checking the proofs of this and I could be in a bit of a fix!) Not a fixation or a fancy of her, maybe a distant regard I suppose. Anyway it was the music that drew me, some of their pop stuff was quite good and in a way at the time some of the melodies spoke to me in an odd sort of way. Music can do that and often does in fact.

The point that I'm getting to, is that the second half of the programme was an expose, as one of the group held a "hidden secret" and this was to be revealed in this programme, and what do you know it involved the girl whom I'd had this "fascination" for. Now most blokes that I knew fancied the blonde girl, I wistfully observed the red haired girl and here she was having some expose revealed about her!

Apparently the so called expose had been revealed back in the late 70's when they were very popular and it was a worry to them and their agents in that it might affect their merchantability etc. Well I never got to hear about it before now so I wondered what it was all about. Apparently it transpired that this girl in ABBA Annifrid Lyngstrom (I hope this is all spelt right!) was not Swedish after all (big news that) like the rest of the band, she was in fact Norwegian. So I thought, what's so startling about all of that? The rest did not really surprise me either as it was revealed that her mother was a young girl when Germany invaded Norway and that her mum had been involved with a German soldier, she was unmarried, she was young, only 17 at the time, and the child Annifrid, was born just after the war finished. On the face of it nothing too sinister so far? So I thought, until this reporter tells us that the German officer was a nazi, OK so that's a bit of something she may want to hide, but worse still, her mum had a very deep regard for him and that of course was seen as fraternisation. It appears that the soldier was recalled to Germany before the pregnancy was known about and he was reported as being killed so she was left to bear and bring up the child herself. Fairly common in wartime I thought naively, except that the nazi's actually planned this sort of thing. Their soldiers were encouraged to "sow their wild oats" with "Aryan stock" irrespective of their marital status to propagate this strong stock that was to constitute the Super race the Germans wished to build.

The war finished and the other German soldiers departed to go home and the rehabilitation of the country started. There then came the retribution upon those who had fraternised with the enemy. Those who had, were punished, and indeed many girls who had consorted with the German soldiers felt the hand of this punishment. Annifrid's mother and grandmother took the view that leaving for Sweden to start a new life was preferable to living in fear of the reprisals being handed out by their country men and woman. Just as well as the "baby factory", and that's how it seemed these German "produced" babies were viewed, were branded as genetically unstable or inferior in fact dangerous due to the German blood in their veins. They were placed into all sorts of institutions by the Norwegian authorities for many years despite there actually being nothing at all wrong with them, excepting they'd been fathered by a German soldier. Annifrids story continues and much more sadness is in her life, there's a biography of her that covers her life much more fully I guess than I've touched on here. The point is though what has happened here? Look at ourselves in what was done. Sure the Germans were wrong, the girls who were part of an occupied country did they actually do wrong? And what of the children, their punishment that was handed out for what they had no part in whatsoever. So were the Norwegians right or wrong to punish the girls, and were they justified in making the children suffer, those produced by the occupying German forces? How many times has this happened, how many times will it happen again all down through history?

This story is only news because it's someone who had fame and fortune albeit for a short period, often the case where the pop industry is concerned. The fact is that many thousands maybe millions have suffered through the millennia in such ways, the war is futile, the vision of the man is futile, and the retribution afterwards, is futile too, dreams are all we have sometimes to help us through such times, but prayer is oh so powerful if only we used it, and used it for the ones that really suffer.

So to another poem and this reflects and calls out about those who suffer and suffer injustice because of the circumstances that have prevailed because of what was brought about by men.

The Million Cries

Through all the years a million cries of anguish rise above this world.
Cries for reasons; why? – cries for sense; cries to ask, why should they die?

The deepest anguish of the mother for the son; father for the son; the daughter; a
child – taken, gone forever?.

The daily working life – the struggle of a war: a conflict; indifference, uncaring
– why do we waste these lives?

Stretched across the countless years a hundred million voices call – and do we
hear their message – repeated by generation, each and every time.

The call, the answer; the reason for it all?; The vastness of the swell of souls be-
yond the comprehension of our poor minds – but.

So is the answer beyond our grasp - our minds our worthiness?
Reach out and touch the only answer - beyond our consciousness, our hope.

12th January 2004

93

You know dreaming can take all sorts of forms, I have been doing my family tree for some years now and since my mother died I have been researching her family. It's all a bit silly as I should have done so when she was still alive, it makes life a lot easier if the person is still around to tell you first hand about things. Nevertheless mum had told me about her dad and the fact that he was a soldier and then when he left the army he went to work in a coal mining village called Polesworth in Warwickshire. The pit was called Pooley Hall and there is a heritage centre there now, giving an insight into their lives all those years ago. I was interested as he died when mum was only 7 and her family faced very tough times as a result of his untimely death, there were no benefits as we know them today in those days.

Whilst visiting the heritage centre I also walked on to the spoil tip, the waste that is heaped up after the coal's been extracted, I felt a huge and overwhelming sense of the hundreds of miners and miners families that had trudged these many miles in search of a livelihood, so much so that I felt compelled to write about them. This next poem was an attempt to encapsulate the dream of their lives I envisaged on that day.

Miners of Pooley Hall

I gazed across the landscape sprawled, before my eyes it lay;
The warming sun, the clouds above, then gently on the trees a breeze did
play.
I'd climbed the hill and looked around for miles my eyes could view,
And yet somehow the sadness here, the years of hardship knew.

Yes right below the carpet here of grass and flowers profuse
It covered up a countless time of human life of laughter, hurt, abuse.
I rubbed my eyes could I see clear, the ground was black right now;
And in the dimness of the light my view I saw the men a walking, quick
and how!

There in among them here and there, a child, a boy between them they
stood too,
How could I see this from my time and from my vantaged view?
A common sight from years past by, the miners here would walk;
Listen carefully right now, the marching to the pit head and all the morn-
ing talk.

The ride within the cage below, as rattled on its way,
Huddled in the cage as one, hardly hearing now, what they all would say;
Talk of life above the ground, playing football, just being in the light;
Times they'd walked within the journeys' cramped and almost taken flight.

Then below the ground, the choking dust, the pitman's daily life,
Above the ground the life, the families the lot for every pitman's wife;
Among the dust a pony's nose that in their pockets for a bite,
And if the pony didn't steal the food within, the mice would look and
might!.

His aching back, his hacking cough, the blackness of the pit,
The way they joked the way they laughed, but this here life is hard, just isn't
it?
My brother worked in here, my father died in here, but always with a hope,
It's strange but often whilst down here, I long for water, and a bar of Fairy
soap.

My child is fair and calls for me, my years beneath the ground,
They long for freedom from these journeys run, but who can earn that extra
pound?;
Times are hard and work was hard, but family life was all we really need;
They prayed release from this dark place we all have spoken and agreed,

Hours have passed the sweat the grime, upon his aching back;
And to the surface rattled upwards his body covered over, all sooty black,
No sun to greet them on the top its warming rays had set so many hours
past;
So homeward bound to rest awhile and strip the outer grime away at last.

The pit heads gone and so are all the blackened faces too,
And back again I stand up here and still to marvel at this view,
How many others stood where I have stood and thought as I have thought,
Not so many, for their lot was no where near to ours, even if they sought.

Think about as they were then and if their life was less?
And look at how our lives are now and do you see a mess?
Their ways were hard and broke the flesh, in poverty the toiled;
Does what we have give more, or are our given gifts all spoiled?.

20th September 2003

I've been back there a couple of times since and really been quite lucky to find a family who knew my Mum as a little girl. They went to the same school and funnily enough the lady that Gen and I saw remembered mothers "beautiful hair". It's quite true she had very beautiful hair, a sort of auburn colour with red highlights in it and we have an old family film with her in it, in her beloved garden, where the sunlight shines upon it and the colours are truly wonderful. She was probably younger than I am now when the film was taken so that's a bit strange for me in a way. Bittersweet too as there was a huge gap between these images and the little old lady I remember struggling with life and death in hospital just before she died.

This is actually leading into the next poem, but I do need to mention the motivation for the poem itself and in doing so in all honesty. You see I had a brother in law, a farmer and quite a chap, larger than life in almost all departments. Gen's sister's husband in fact, a man that I had immense difficulty in truly liking hardly suprising given that we come from very different backgrounds and cultures and why should we be good friends, we had no blood ties or reasons for being so.

Gen's family are Welsh, Welsh speaking and are proud of their roots, nothing wrong at all with that I think, but I did have a difficulty with this man whether he'd have been Welsh or not. Notwithstanding, he was good company and was a first class practical joker, a Church man and strong in the community within which he lived, and died I think.
He'd been badly injured in a car crash many years before, we'd all suspected that a lesser man would never have survived the dreadful injuries that he sustained, but he did and as far as I can make out he never complained about his lot where this was concerned, even though it made his job of hill farming a darned sight more difficult than you could imagine.

Funny thing is that we'd had our run ins and had our times of peace and in a way I tried hard to be "friends" with him. Problem is that we neither of us had much in common and I suspect that often I tried too hard to be what was "expected" rather than being me, just plain old me. He'd probably thought a lot more of me than he did, had I done just that. Trouble is that dreamers often try to be all things to all men, and the results are often pretty dire, I think that in this case it certainly was.

The problem is that he developed cancer late in life and although he fought hard to recover from it, we all learned that the cancer had arrived in his liver and the prognosis was not good at all. In fact it was clearly a terminal issue,

I never discovered if he had knowledge of this or not, but right now, a few years or so after his death it seems quite pointless whether or not he did. The major issue to me was that I saw this huge man, both physically and mentally, reduced to a shell of his former self, not even when he was struck by a car and smashed very badly did he look as poorly as this.

We were visiting a nearby town as a re-union sort of visit actually, it was a place we'd been through on the canals and found a nice pub with good food and accommodation so we'd said we'd return and re-visit.

Whilst there Gen and I thought that we'd visit Gen's sister and her husband as this place was quite close. Plus we were worried about his health and the fact that he seemed to be going down very quickly. The fact is he died a few days after our visit and I find myself feeling very emotional about that visit for I have to say that once in both our lifetimes I actually felt that I was on a level playing field with him, and here he was so close to death. I do not feel any guilt in any way right now, we were so different as people, but in the circumstances the levelling that we had was God given as we parted as friends and he will be embraced by God despite what we, as mere humans felt for each other. I did however express my feelings in a poem that was a reflective, not only for my brother in law but the way that we often have to witness the demise of those whom we love and those whom we aspire to love but often have the greatest difficulty in reaching, I give to all the poem, "A Glance -- for Emyr".

A Glance

"I caught the glimpse of Jesus' face, a moment in my haunted place,
The life that drained was clear to see, but soon the spirit from the flesh was
free:

The toil the suffering of this place, replaced completely through His ever
loving grace:
We saw the Christ like struggle clear, we lost him, gained Him even now
He's near:

The broken flesh the sweat the blood, the suffering of the flesh we should:
See through Christ it was His gift, the spirit ascends with Him the praise
we lift.

From Life to Life with God we go, the risen Lord our route did show:
Alleluia for our King, Messiah a hundred million voices will forever sing:

Christ the Flesh, the risen Lord is near, feel His presence we have no fear:
That glimpse, that glance, the face I saw, It was the Christ that opened up
the door."

19th June 2003

After his passing we had reflected on his age and it was a shock how the passage of time had occurred, I know that my mother said years ago that time was not for wasting, and yet as a youngster the days seemed so long and that time took so long to pass. The interminable waiting for school holidays, and then the long summer days that I dreamed all the way through. Now as I approach the "golden" 60 years of age marker I feel that life is all too fast and everything is passing by so quickly!

Just to demonstrate this, I was at a Churchwardens meeting some time ago and have to admit that I don't find them the most riveting of occasions and so I started to drift as I often do!! (Or even dream, could you believe this??) How many times have you been at an event, a meeting or maybe as a child waiting for the adults to finish the boring chats they had? Well does this little poem say anything?

Time

Hear the ticking of the clock, time just passing by
That gentle sound from just afar, time slipping by without a sigh;
Every tick a moment, fragment of your life
Listen hear it as it slips so gently by, your life.
Chimes that tell the hour of day
Tells you of your life that passed that way.

Time the thief of life, stealing minutes stealing hours each and every day
If I had more I'd do so much, often we all say.
From afar I hear those minutes as they pass forever
Lost in time eternity they will return not ever;
Never squander precious moments from your life ahead
Invest them wisely those hours and days as Jesus he had said.

Written at a Churchwardens meeting 4ᵗʰ December 2003

Chapter Seven
A Change of Direction?

I was mentioning in the last chapter about the fact that time was creeping up on me and how I was getting a bit phased by the way time seemed to be rushing by. Mostly this was because the life style that I had, I say had, because something changed whilst writing this book. It is probably because I've taken such a long time to write the thing that life is passing us all by, and I begin to think that I'll never finish it!! So subsequently things have moved on.

Well what's happened is, I changed my job. All of a sudden I apply for this job in Hinckley where I live and suddenly I get it and suddenly I should have loads more time to do things!! Well it never quite works out like that does it? I might be able to go to work an hour and a bit later, but I get up later and don't maximise the time I ought to have, plus I spend more time lounging around now which is probably good for the stress levels but pretty poor for getting important jobs done!! Another thing that's changed is that whilst I mentioned earlier about Cursillo and the friend who'd lead one of these week ends, well I've been chosen to lead one now!

I said that I was taking too long to write this book, events keep happening and I'm just not recording them quick enough!!

So what about this changing of direction? Well, I was chosen to lead the LAC number 22 at Launde Abbey and this was a piece of work that I wanted to do, but was very scared of, for I am not a very organized person and organization is a keynote of the success of the weekends. Furthermore I find that I get very stressed too if I am trying hard to make something happen that means a lot to people and is Gods work too. These weekends are wonderful experiences and if done properly and followed up in the way that they should be, make us very strong Christians. Capable of accepting the challenges of the world and the failings of that world, but doing it as God would want us to do.

We fail, I fail, the humanness is always there, but so is God in all the things that we do and aspire to in His name. I was very stressed out by the planning and execution of this weekend, a lot of changes took place during the planning stage and also during the weekend itself. I was a bit upset by some of the things that happened but learned that this is what the challenge is all about, meeting them head on but with Gods greatness and the faith in Him, mountains can be moved. Physically I felt tired and there were times I was off hand or struggling to make the grade, but this is where God provides, he provided me with fellow Christians all around who understood and were the rocks upon which His son Jesus Christ built His Church, His body on earth. So the weekend would be a success. Not a success in material means or by how I'd performed, no, what was done was to channel through me, in assembling a team that He knew would be good to work with me, around me and make sure that we all gave to the participants the message the love the need to be His apostles.

The gift that He bestows too, though, is that those who serve as staff members also receive, not in the same way but are inspired and drawn to His light, His Love so that they are renewed and seek to continue serving as a Christian wanting to do His work and to keep the body of Christ active and meaningful in the world we live in today.

Whilst the planning of the weekend was taking place, one of the staff team and I talked about the pitfalls of serving the Lord and how we never seem to understand the way ahead, I sent this fine lady a poem to help, it's the "Along a City Street" which is nearer the front of the book. She said that it was significant to her and the place she was in right now. The funny thing is that I too have had some difficulty in understanding where I need to be and what I should be doing next. My disappointments are no where near the same as this lady but it never ceases to amaze me how we get knocked and then something happens or someone happens, just when you need it and the path seems to clear a little again.

I looked back over the last three years or so and thought about this "change of direction" and see that I moved from St Mary's Church in Hinckley to St Margaret's Church in Stoke Golding (a small village a few miles from where

I live) became a Church Warden, went on the "Exploring Christian Life and Faith" course, staffed again on a Cursillo weekend, then lead a Cursillo weekend. What has He got in store for me? I have absolutely no idea right now but I just know that whatever it is He will give me the load just heavy enough just testing enough for me to do. And the funny thing is that I know that it's right, but keep beavering away where I am and the changes will be what is required.

I will be helping in the leading of services in our Church from 2005 onwards, our new Rector has five Churches in the benefice called the Fenn lanes which includes our Church in Stoke Golding, but she is one person and if we want to have a service in all the Churches every week, well someone has to be around to help and that's down to the lay people and "Changes of Direction".

So here comes a time to have a poem to help us on the way. It's about the wonder of the things around us:

The Wonder

I see the petals on the flower, as perfect in the rays of light;
I watch the darting movements of the butterfly in flight:
And wonder fills my soul.

I sit and watch you as we talk, the gift we share is clear
The sunlight gently shines upon your face and brings you very near:
And wonder fills my soul.

The trust the love we're blessed with is flowing through us all;
And all we think sometimes is clear, we fear how we will fall:
And wonder fills my soul.

You sit across from me and though we talk of how we feel;
The truth in what we say not feel, tell me honest tell me real:
Then wonder fills my soul.

The time it takes to know someone, to love someone, how long?
Write the words, speak them loud, sing them in a song;
The wonder fills my soul.

Don't be afraid, don't feel confused, just say the words you mean;
If from the soul, the heart you speak you really will be seen;
The wonder fills your soul.

Hold out your hand, place yours in mine and promise as we're taught;
The way we feel the way we are, we'll never feel caught;
Then feel the wonder when it fills our souls.

Through life, through death, remember always of your oath;
We need in life this earthly life the strength of each of both:
Now feel the wonder as it enters in our souls.

Hear gently as I speak these words to you, for I am just like you;
The one who knows us all so well speaks through me and you;
Now can you feel the wonder of Him in your very soul?.

25th August 2003

105

You know the trouble with changes in direction, it often gives rise to reflection! Reflection of your past or considering what you've done, the right bits and inevitably the wrong bits, life's a bit like that and unless you're very lucky and very blessed, there may well be all sorts of murky bits or regrets in the journey through life you've made so far. I know I certainly have, and its at times like these I tend to start wondering about where I've been and why has this or that happened, and the pain that some of it induces. I had this wonderful idea that by becoming a Christian overnight (or nearabouts) I'd change and become that wonderful spirit filled genuinely nice bloke that I always really wanted to be and never was. Around 1993 or so when my dad died my life really was going nowhere, I had a few friends and went on holidays where I met nice people and in some ways kept in touch with them. This was all very comfy and I hope those people that Gen and I have kept in touch with are reminded of that short spell pf time we shared on the holiday, but friendship? Was it? Is it? And what of the other friends we saw often? My family, Gen's family? Was I honest in my friendship and what of it anyway?

I have said before that when my dad died I met the Vicar of St Mary's Brian Davis (Canon in fact) and how impressed I was with his handling of dads funeral and his concern shown for us as a family, irrespective of the fact that none of us (with the exception of my wife) were Church goers, maybe he could see a sales pitch here, but it was never that evident and his kindness saw me through not only that time, but also when my mother passed so awfully with cancer. I also met as a result many members of St Mary's Church and especially Jane Atkins.

Jane was on a journey too when I first met her, still is I believe like many of us, but she took the change of direction in her life so seriously and strove for the clergy. I admired her then and do so still, because of not what she's doing but how she's doing it.

When I started writing the "Christian" poetry and wrote a little book which did the rounds some years ago, and I never tried honestly to get it published, maybe I should have done (maybe I might if this lot turns out OK) the contents were in fact put together by the encouragement of an old school friend and Jane (and one or two others) who obviously saw what I could not, a gift in the words that were being written. I suspect that some are very primitive in their construction and the scholars would have something to say about them, but they are written from the heart, the soul and for the sake of the God that is our Father.

Returning to the friends and what I said above about "friends", well some
of the "established" ones left, and keep in touch from time to time, but the
Church ones never fail to surprise me with their constancy despite my inat-
tentiveness as I dither all over the place trying to do what I thought God
wanted from this rather "damaged" and sinful person. I had always dreamt
(see the poem on that earlier on!) of being able to do great feats of work!!!.
Becoming a councillor was a naïve belief that this could be a platform to be
honourably able to make change and help people in a positive way. Was I ever
so naïve!, was I ever so crushed by the general public, no, not everyone caused
me pain and heartache, but the route was so difficult and so time consuming
I despaired often and very nearly allowed it to cause my health to suffer ir-
reparably. It did in fact, but luckily with the friends around me, whether they
knew it or not, I came through two very sticky times of my life. Both could
have resulted in my complete destruction, not only as a person, but more
importantly as a Christian person.

The trouble is I still cannot continue without some element of my "past
life" haunting me and causing me to wonder if I really have or can change
as I thought God wanted me to. Anyway, back to the book issue, I grandly
thought I could get the little book published and start to earn money that
way, so I could do "good deeds" without the encumbrance of work and before
I became too old to be "young enough" to understand and open enough to
help the cause I thought that God had there for me. Well I was never and am
still not, organised enough to get the book or any paperwork together to stop
working or "do good". So I mused about winning a huge sum of money on
the lottery, that would help - boy could I do some good with that!! And in
any case wouldn't that be OK to pray for?, I'd be doing Gods work with cash
wouldn't I? the trouble is that's the easy route isn't it?

I still have the lack of confidence, the troubled mind, the dithering about the
change of direction in that it's in Gods hands, trust Him as your real friend
and stop hoping for the impossible, do something that is, and this is where
the truth lies. Jesus took 12 disciples with no huge cash pile, no circus, no big
advertisements, and no big campaign machinery He just went and accepted
people, warts and all, and took His Father's love to them all and He didn't
have lottery wins or other such things to aid His campaign at all -- just Him
and the word of God, with Love. So why is my change of direction causing
me so much of a problem? Partially because I'm human and partly because do
I listen? Do I try to listen to what He tells us, me or anyone for that matter?
Instead of wishing and hoping for the "comfort" zone, join His zone without

comfort, without the cosseted lifestyles, without money – but with Him as your guiding light in your change of direction.

Poem time again, this time and old one!

Understanding

Do you understand the meaning of it all?
Does your mind take it , or does it just fall?
What am I talking of what's this gibberish flow?
Should I listen, think or merely go?.

I ask myself in my little way, what do I know?
What does my mind say and understand of thoughts that inwardly grow?.
Did I know what you were talking about just then?
Did I understand the words in my mind now and again?

Who speaks to me quietly and frightens my poor existence?
Why do I shun the words pretend nothings there, non-existence!

Speak to me of your world and what you believe;
I listen half hearted and ignore most and then I relieve.

You talk in half truths and never reach the real me,
Why do we do that? Talk meaningful but no truth do you see.
Ask what goal it is that you seek, what goal?
Understanding what we want, what you want, is it in your soul?

Who has the key? Where is the lock? Who knows the code?
And on and on you increase your own wearisome load.
Only when you feel the understanding, the truth come from your own human tongue,
Will you really know the comfort of the Holy one's song.

19th April 2002

So changes of direction, recent changes we are experiencing are the lay lead services in our local church and the fact that we have formed a "worship group" which exists to help with the services that our rector can't take because she's elsewhere. The growing in that group is becoming very clear and that the direction is changing and that this is going to be quite challenging not so much for us now, but the more "established" members of the church. We now need to be able to carry them with us as we seek new horizons and try to draw new people to the church, maybe ones who'd not considered the Christian way or maybe had but not had the nudge they needed to make that commitment and join in. Quite a balancing act when you look at the way that some churches struggle with the way forward especially in times that challenge the churches and especially the Church of England. Being able to share the changes and introduce them so that everyone is benefited is the greatest challenge we all face in a world that seems to have turned its back on Christian ethics and the rule of life we need to stick to.

Funnily enough with me changing my job recently and now working locally, with this new environment I thought that I'd enjoy I found that it's not quite what I thought that it would be. I found that the young person I work with has had perhaps the most difficult of times in the may years that she's been with this firm and the general perspective of the employers and the people that use the establishment shows a very odd view of how life is, and can be. The problem is that I worked on the basis that the grass would be greener etc etc, and often that's not quite the case is it! So changes of direction can sometimes not work in your favour! The problem is though that I spent so many years in one firm I tended to forget and indeed never experienced what was going on in other firms, until one day I went on a business management course and met peers from other companies. It was a shock for us all on that course to a certain extent, as although we all worked in similar ways and used similar management tools for our various companies, our way of using these procedures and working ethics differed quite a bit. That which we thought totally acceptable in one organisation was frowned upon in another even though as I said, the principles taken from the management text books gave us to believe that we were both right.

Interpretations of the "instructions" in different ways and by differing people accounted for the considerable variations in the work cultures. Some we reconciled had just completely bent the rules to suit themselves and that often happens, but a lot just took their interpretations and used that as the basis of the structure. I was thinking about that when I was deep in conversation about the Bible texts and the way we understand them. Some of them I see completely differently to others and I was worried that I had got it absolutely wrong until one day someone said to me "no that's exactly how I see it too!". I was relieved as I really began to wonder if I was totally on the wrong track in this Christian malarkey and condemned straight away because I couldn't see the same meanings as a number of others, not that there were huge differences, just variations on the overall theme big enough to set us apart when discussing Biblical texts. I made the comparison therefore of the way workplace ethics based on one set of rules can be interpreted in one way as can most important texts of the Bible. Maybe it's the way and maybe this is a clumsy comparison that we should have this freedom of thought when establishing how we live or work and how we believe when seeking Jesus.

Changes in direction can therefore be brought about by the perspectives we see and judge things by and also about how we mature, again be it in the workplace, our lives in general or in the spiritual journey we undertake throughout our lives.

The next poem is probably a bit out of context here as it looks at how much love we need or deserve when we are faced with loss, changes and the yearning for the 'lostness' of our lives.

How Much Love?

My eyes mist over and cloud my view,
I wish I could, still look at you.
The scene the fields, the flowers here,
Touch your hand and feel you near.

The closeness of you next to me
As once we were, Oh yes I still can see.
A night so clear as moon light shines
For you alone my heart still pines

As breezes play upon your hair
I still upon your face will stare
I loved you then, I love you now
My heart is still the same somehow.

Our hearts stay young but we grow old
This is a story often told
So sleep in heaven eternal one
And I'll pretend that you've not gone

I'll tell myself the lie some more
Until I see you clearly on that shore
That smallish step between us now
Will seem like nothing when I know how.

2nd July 2002

Chapter Eight
Pain Along the way.

Something occurred to me after putting the last Chapter together and that was about the difficulty we have and the pains endured as we go about our Christian lives. I mentioned in the last chapter about leading a Christian Cursillo weekend and although that was a wonderful experience and has helped in a great many ways, I had my own tribulations during the lead up and indeed during the weekend itself. I had prayed and asked for help but the problems still came and I wondered about that because if this was Gods will, why did things go wrong and why didn't everyone else understand that this was a job of work for God and couldn't they all see that I was doing His will and so on! I wondered too about this friend of mine, Jane who had been our curate in the benefice I serve and then became able to apply for stipendiary jobs. She'd been having a real time of it, someone I think who has a real gift to share and will carry the word of God in such a fine way, but could she get a job?
I thought that this was really unfair, and what is the good Lord thinking about? She should be strolling into a job.

Well its not quite like that is it? Jane knew that too although she was having to take this on the chin so to speak and it must have been testing on her faith. As I say I was musing about all of this until recently we had an AID's awareness service at St Mary's Church (our old Church in Hinckley) where I was asked to contribute some poetry or words in the service along with other very talented musicians and folks who had come from doing work in Africa with people affected by the disease. It's a bit daunting when you try to put words together to express what you think about a disease that has stricken so many and is still largely regarded as being something affecting "other" people and

"Gays". Well it's not true in either case any more even if it was originally and it gave me a lot of thought and not much time to assemble some words that would do justice to an epidemic that is affecting more and more people all over the world and still there is no cure really in sight.

So with that in mind I also reflected on the conflict that is still going on in Iraq and the continuing problems in Israel and Palestine, and then just to try the very faith of all religions, a Tsunami wave hits the near east over Christmas time 2004 and destroys towns centres and the death toll is being speculated at over 150,000 dead, the final figure we may never know. So what do we say to each other about how much God cares for us all. My reaction initially was to start looking into the book of Job to see if there's a hint in that book that I missed. I'm not even going to try and make any suggestions, merely give you a couple of the poems I did for the AID's awareness service and ask you to think about that, for a start.

Why me?

I sit here looking at a world, a world that has rejected me.
I try to see the reason why and still I am rejected.

My skin is any colour, my race is any race and my belief is just the same as yours!
And yet you still reject me out of hand.

I say to God I am your child and ask Him to accept me, forgive me, love me, does He hear my honest plea?

I lie here looking at a world that condemns me, looks at me as something less and something tarnished,
And yet my Lord still loves me, I know he does, I'm sure He does.

What is my crime, what is my problem such that all the world no longer views me in any other way,
Than human garbage, and what was my crime what did I do?

My time is near I feel the ebb from all my vitals and still I feel no one is understanding, believing:
Hearing my call for help! The way my very existence calls to mankind to listen, to understand, to love me.

And as my life is ended, snuffed out prematurely, for the very thing that takes me from this world is spreading inexorably,
Across this world of Gods, this world of man, hear my call, my existence, my passing.

Pray for me and all those who go across the great division between the ones who are and who are no longer.

Understand as life dawns on the horizon of suffering, the hidden life taker that roams the earth,
Listen to the silence of the mass that is unheard and unknown.

23rd October 2004

I was not able to hold the need to write the next one, as I have seen in my own minds eye the pain that is in the heart of the ones that come to God, sometimes for the first time imploring Him to help, asking for the faith they need and wondering what will be the outcome and will they ever learn to trust and be as one with Him?

And so,

My Prayers – Alone

I sit here in this Church, my hands clasped tight together, I pray to God
and ask, "What is it that is happening, why was my child chosen to die this
way?"
My tears flow down my cheeks, I choke upon the feeble words that utter
from my mouth.

I do not understand my God, I do not understand.

The evil creeping death that takes away my child, denies me of the happi-
ness the fulfilment of the years ahead, I pray for deliverance I ask out loud
for mercy; but no, nothing is there, the end is coming soon.

I raise my head, I open up my eyes, eyes stinging with the tears of passion,
emotion, hatred, love; what is it deep within my soul that weeps that cries
out for the mercy for my child's life.

I tried Lord, I tried! But why did my child choose to ignore my pleas, ig-
nore my words when asking:
For care, for thought -- mind what you do, where you go, my child my
little golden haired one.

Who now lies so mortally wounded by this invasive virus, this unseen killer
that stalks the earth and brings down the young the old, the good the evil.
But why my child I ask I beg, my heart goes cold why oh why? I call out for
help for a miracle for Gods deliverance, grace – but all I hear is silence.

A million voices a million mothers cry out from all the world, a fever pitch
of love of anguish at the dawn of this evil that invades our lives.
With pride they see the child with love and fond affection as this child is
grown and soon becomes their own:

Their way, their freedom to choose whatever they want or wish -- careful
my little one, brush the hair, kiss the cheek.
What can I do, where can I go, what has this world done to my child of
God.

My prayer is answered by a vision – the world that took another child, a
son, a mother wringing hands in anguish – my son, my little one.
Taken from her even though His life was precious more to her than all the
jewels and gold that earth can offer give and take away.

She too did not have a choice a way and she saw her son her child taken --
taken by those, by the world that called for Him to die.
But by His great sacrifice, the mother who watched and wept and knows
the sacrifice and knows that He redeems, and knows that He is with those
who are condemned, and we must learn and hear Him still.

30th November 2004

The words are directed for the thoughts about the AID's or other infections that kill. Some in fact are nowhere near as deadly as the AID's virus but because of conflict or man's indifference or the greed of some, kill just as many because the drugs they need cannot get to them because the money is fraudulently spirited away or the food or medical supplies never find their way to those that need it, and who are they? The weakest, the least able to survive the children the women, all because of the ideals of mere human mortal men who say that the sacrifice is worth it for the cause, whatever that turns out to be. In some cases it's because of our belief too, because my way is right and you need to change because our God is always right, try telling that to a mother whose child hangs lifeless in her arms, or a Tsunami victim, that lone child stripped of all their family and belongings, who will love me now?

So what of the words that we want to help us through this disaster? What do we say to God? What should we say to those who despite the natural worlds grief and turning on itself they continue to bomb maim and kill innocents who are but a few hundred miles away.

Take a choice then and see what it means overall:

Take my Life?

You deny the right for me and would take my life: -- and what if your life
was taken by an earth in convulsions of its life?

Would you say that your god had taken it? -- Or taken up your soul?

What was your gods purpose of the great convulsion that had taken all
those lives? of all races, colours, of all faiths -- so different -- their only
commonality? -- they were human beings.

And yet you say that you must take the life away from those who are not of
your creed, or colour, or race or believe the same as you, to save the world
because your god is right!

Can you not see through this veil of smoke this lie that divides us all from
each other? -- the God who is the one, lives for all, and loves and saves for
all: despises not you or me!

Our colour or our race – or because we cannot love each other for the
other: -- and yet when needed we are together and we can give in greatness
when moved because of threat and common danger.

Why can we not see the common danger in our commonness of being torn
apart by belief that should be; what should call us, always to be together.
We suffer together as mortal human beings, we suffer so much and feel for
all who suffer.

And we can be generous, so generous, our hearts go out and we are on fire
to be beside the ones who are destroyed! -- But when will the time be ripe
for you and I and all the ones destroyed or different?

Or have a mind set aside from yours – because our God made us all this
way – so different, so special, so individual. So we can hold a joy, -- a won-
derous moment, a sadness, a desperation – our suffering.

And when will you see the suffering you cause is not of our Gods hand, and
not of His almighty mind or purpose! -- but it is of you and I: Imperfect,
impulsive, human and, different: -- Just as He made us.

Just so we can be what He had always in mind for us -- to be separate, to be apart, to be different – but to love one another. To love each other for that's His way – and our way, as different as we are.

As different in our culture, tongue, our ways: the colour of our skin our race -- but pray we do as one -- we cannot deny our prayers are always to our Father in Heaven.
Despite our differences we have, we are still all the same.

3rd January 2005

The Tsunami horror as it unfolded over the Christmas time and New Year did make an awful lot of people dig deep into their pockets and send the most generous donations to the stricken areas. My wife and I did too, but the over-riding thought in my mind is that the money will help now, but what about next year when the spotlight is off? You see Ethiopia has been a country in famine for years as have many of the African states trouble enough without having to handle the AID's problem, so what of that? Again the role of God is brought out and I have wondered how we should see His love in all of this pain and anguish?

Closer to home too, I hear of old friends and relations stricken with all man-ner of ailments and cancers, major tragedies in their families, does God really hear us? Or are we not talking to Him any more? Answers to all of these are too much for anyone to contemplate and give rich pickings for those who do not believe and choose to use them as examples of why the loving God either does not exist, or at best has deserted us or is not listening because, well because of what?

I was watching a DVD copy of a video the other night, it's the Pink Floyd story, a band that I like and have done so for many years, along with a few others too but the interviews in this TV documentary of the key members were what struck me. You see they split up after many years together and one of the band members, Roger Waters is regarded rather, as the one that was behind it all. Whether or not he was, is immaterial here, what is the interesting bit was that during the interviews he said that he had been told by his mother to be getting ready for life, schooling for instance, making ready for that time when life would begin. He said that he'd been suddenly awakened to realise that it had started already and that he was living it . The fact is, it had started and he wasn't quite ready for that. I understood that because I had held this belief as a youngster that I didn't understand at say 5 years old but I'd be OK at 10 say. But when I became 10, I was no further forward in a way and so I thought, well when I'm 15 I'll understand more.

This went on very much like Roger Waters thoughts until I was 18 and I really did have a crisis, something I mentioned earlier in the book and that was I faced my own mortality. But much worse I thought that I couldn't understand things at this age and that as I became 21 and a man, I'd become capable of understanding about life and all about Life.

Well, I was wrong, and I discovered that life actually became far more com-plicated, and that I was unable to understand it, and the people in it, even less so. I hadn't realised that people will exploit other people irrespective of what they are, and if you let them "in" they would use that knowledge to their own advantage, so the learning curve started all over again only on a far more difficult level. You see being "adult" gave me no more rights or understanding, in fact it gave me even less. I hadn't found the Christian friends and understood the way that they will forgive, and even more important, how God forgives.

I had held a huge desire, a real wish to be "musical" when I was younger, I wanted to be in a pop group and flirted with the idea but never had the real guts to go out and "do it". A number of friends from school did and I tried once to "manage" a group. I was not even good at it and the one or two venues I got for them were fraught and it cost me money at the end of it all because I wasn't hard nosed enough to be able to make money. I marvelled at guitar players and the first one that I was aware of was Hank Marvin of the Shadows. School mates also held him in high regard and so it was he who had us all wandering around strumming cricket bats or tennis rackets. The music that he was involved in was instrumental so there were no lyrics to "get in the way". That was a bit of a funny thing because the music they made invoked lots of thoughts of what the music held for us. I remember well the emotions I felt when I first heard "Wonderful Land" which the Shadows released in 1962, and then "Theme for Young Lovers", a piece of music that my mum liked too. I listened to lyrics in songs by the late great Buddy Holly and when he was killed in 1959 that had a very difficult moment in my life as "famous people" didn't die, not at that age anyway. The lyrics didn't seem to have any great effect though, apart from the odd one or two especially after he died.

Much later on I worked for Decca records and I heard the music of the Moody Blues, the lyrics of their songs seemed to have a message in them whether or not they did is not important, to me they seemed to tell me things. Mike Pinder was one of the founder members and he left the band in something like 1978 or 79. He made a couple of solo records and the message was clear, here too was a man searching for the truth, the lyrics told me that very obviously. I couldn't seem to realise the message though, it would take a long journey and much help before I got anywhere near where I am now. It was about now that I found Pink Floyds album "Dark Side of the Moon". I didn't like it much at first, I found the words difficult and the meanings tough too. But there seemed to be some empathy with what they were trying to say and where I was trying to go.

A few words now to reflect upon which I actually wrote as a part of the group of poems that I was preparing for the AID's awareness service and seem to help at the point I'd reached in this part of the book.

The Returning

Splashing back and forth, rushing over pebbles, soaking in the sand, the sea
as it comes and goes, the tide that washes back and forth;
The way I see our lives as water rushing on the beach, it surges forward
strong and forceful – rushes back and disappears when drawing back into
the sea as ebbs the tide.

Our lives which start as strong and youthful full of hope and full of antici-
pation, full of expectation of what this world has for us all;
Our will our freedom, our want and thirst for all the gifts, the temptations,
the things available for us – to have to take to feel to rush into – just like
the waves upon that shore.

The fears of what there is for us all – when tempted – take and care less for
the consequences and then regret what it was that was so evil oh so bad and
what has it given to all those others?

Those who knew not what we bequeathed to them – our foolishness our
naivety our ignorance condemned them all; and me and you who were not
able to contain or understand or care enough to feel, to listen properly for
caution.

To love to protect, because we did not want to hold our desires back be-
cause we surged like all those waves upon the shore – but yet if we could
but believe, if we can see the waves as tides turn, the water runs, returns as
ever it will do.

As that returns to the mighty sea, even though we do so wrong and listen
little and care so little; have the right to have our way – we too like the re-
turning tides will always be going back, like those waves to the great eternal
home saved for all who sin and all who fail, He who fails us not nor ever.

23rd October 2004

Pink Floyd still held a grip on my musical taste and I guess that even though I'd locked onto some of Graham Kendrick's musical genius I was still happier with Pink Floyd and the incredible riffs that were prevalent in their music. I was quite shocked in 1987 or so when I heard a "new" album called "A Momentary Lapse of Reason". It was a new move for them as by this time they'd lost Roger Waters and many thought they'd be washed up without him as Roger had tended to write most of the lyrics for the songs previously. One song stuck with me from this album and it's well worth a listen, for even if wasn't intended to have any Christian message in it, it certainly said something to me. It's called "On the Turning Away" and it's a ballad. I suppose that copyright precludes me from including the lyrics in here but it has some of the strongest words that we could ever say about how we treat each other and then "Turn away".

I suppose that by now you're thinking "what is this to do with the Tsunami and God's role in that". Well probably very little except whatever happens to any of us, and whatever we think God is saying or not saying, it's very hard to ignore the messages that arrive everyday in one form or another during our lives. I have just charted a path during my trek towards God, a musical one which is just a part of my understanding or not as the case might be, but it is no less a path that I have walked in trying to reach out to God and to get my life nearer to what He wants of me. There are no answers on the path, frankly I did not and still don't expect to hear answers, the Tsunami, Iraq, Ireland, Israel, African conflicts AID's anything that you can throw at me or any other Christian. No answers are there, but Gods love still comes through as the way that humans react with humans is shown through the way that we do Christ's work even though it looks that God has forsaken us, He never does and never has, but we just don't know the answers and even if we live to be 100 years old we'll never have the answers in this life here, it was never intended.

I was working away in Rugeley which I have mentioned a number of times in this book, and I was unhappy there.
I have had the greatest difficulty settling in any work maybe because I have had no clear intent as to what I should have done and the lack of real courage to take the route I should have done years ago. This comes out sometimes in the way that we are, we all have some great action or some great feat we would have liked to have done or achieved and I have been frustrated by that, so much so that this frustration spills over into downright hostility. Especially if I'm wrong and I do something that is clearly a cover up for that inability or error and then lies! Nothing hurts more than when the lie is uncovered and then seeking to absolve the need to tell that untruth, and the feeling of

hopelessness when it gets out of hand and you get deeper into the lying and the cover up. I did such a thing once and I still shift uneasily about it now, so much so that I had to write down the fact, and then as I glanced into the Bible one day and read in James' letter about the "tongue" and it's horrible abilities, well judge this poem and see if you can understand where I was at that moment.

Speak to Me (Peters Poem)

Peter, speak to me, tell me what it felt like, after you denied our Lord? As
I have spoken, used words that tumbled, disjointed, full of lies and spite,
from this mouth of mine. I feel dejected, disgusted, as if I drove the nails
home hard and watched His gentle face.

Did you feel so utterly bereft, so lost, so incapable of forgiveness?

Did you run away and cry and sob, and break your heart, a heart given by
the Lord for joy and sharing, broken by the sin of fear and lies?

Did you peer deep in those eyes and feel the human pain as whip lash laid
across His flesh, as nails were driven deep through the flesh, and human
pain went far beyond the limit that a human frame can take?

Did the spoken word which tumbled easily from those lips taste as bitter as
the soured wine, or of the sweated mouth of someone pushed beyond en-
durance before the final act of pain and humiliation?

Tell me Peter after you were broken by these words you spoke, did the
spirit stay within you? Did the sharing of the Christian brothers, sisters
all around, did the Lords word in your soul sustain you, forgive you? And
when you went forth with forgiveness from that gentle man of Naza-
reth…………………………………did you see redemptions path?

20th June 2004

In a way it was easier to write that down and then ask the Father for forgiveness, maybe I should be more of a Christian and try to be more honest and Christ like, but I am what I am, a sinner and deeply flawed, but we all are to a greater or lesser extent. But that's what is God's way, He knows that, He knew that before we did and don't look for the reasons we'll never know, well not in this life as I said above it's just not meant to be. So I just keep writing, is it for me? Is it for God? Have the words said anything to you? I don't need to know, it would be nice to know, but if the purpose is truly Gods will then I don't need to know at all, you will know and God will too. That's the important part of it all.

I wrote a poem some time ago and it was one of those that as usual just tumbled out onto the paper and was there right in front of me, another one that went on the computer ready for the book, whenever this epic will get completed, as that's how it's felt these many months as I've struggled to get the time the effort to get the words on the paper. The poems seemed easy by comparison, then where to put them in the text? Well after the sort of issues raised in this chapter I guess that this one is as pertinent as any and was for me a way of looking at things that were really beyond me and must have something to say when we ask where is God when the hurts start.

Where are You?

You are not here they said, You were at peace.

I can no longer touch You, see You -- You have gone from here;
And all that's left is just a memory which fades with time.

Again I open up my eyes and look and still I cannot see You there; I strain
my eyes to hear You, but still You are not heard; I stretch my hands and
arms for You but still I cannot feel You there.

But I see You in the summer sun, the trees and woodlands near and far; I
see You in the summer morning when the earth is fresh and new, and I hear
You in the birds on wing and raindrops as they fall;

I hear You in the rushing brook and stream I touch You every day as I feel
the earth beneath my feet and feel the softest breeze upon my face.

You are not gone, but alive in all things I can perceive within the world I
live; You wait for me when time will call us all to be with You, and when a
tear will no longer wet my face and aching heart not yearn for You.

So as You wait for us beyond the place we cannot see or hear or touch: let
us see you in the wonders that surround us and hear Your gentle voice in
times we need You most, and if it pleases You, touch our hearts and souls
until we are with you.

23rd June 2004

In ending this chapter I wondered of all the remaining poems that I had currently, which would be the right one to finish with. I had a thought that I ought to sit down and compose a special one and then finish off, but I didn't have any inspiration so again I looked in the pile of papers that constitutes the poems held in reserve!.

I also thought about this "Pain Along the Way" business again and considered what it means to most of us. Is it a fear of what is going to happen to us? To our family or as I have said previously the acts of nature in Tsunami's or illnesses, which affects everyone globally, but you can close your eyes and minds to that and pretend it doesn't affect you so why do you worry. I worry about my relationship with God and Jesus and when I do the wrong things I have "Pain Along the Way" because I am not following Christ's message and although I want to, often my free will, my stubbornness, just plain me prevents this.

So what if Jesus wanted to talk to you and calm you about the worries of life and the way we're all going, for no matter what we all think we know that we all return to the home He has for us, so why can't we have some sort of understanding of that too? I wrote the next poem ages ago, didn't really think I'd use it because it was me asking about whether or not I'd know Jesus if He spoke and how would He speak anyway.

Who Just Spoke to Me?

One night I dreamt and saw a light
So bright it was I had a fright
I woke from slumber sweating scared
What was this dream should I have cared?

My mind still reels my senses whirled
As if in limbo I'd been hurled
A voice from just beyond the brilliant glare
Said "fear not Child, just hold your stare

A face a form began to show
Should I run off where could I go
The voice was clear and firmer now
I could hear the breath I cried and how

It said to me to look beyond the voice
The fear I had I had no choice
And then the face began to clear
The voice it also seemed so near

I shuddered but let out no sound
The visage cleared and the face was found
I was no longer lost, I didn't need to plea,
It was My Lord just there, who spoke to me.

10 October 2002

Chapter Nine
Finishing Off!!

As I got to where I thought the last chapter should be, I got my wife Gen, to look at the text so far and I looked at the poems left over, some of which I thought were worthy of the last chapter and others that I wasn't sure of. Part of the thoughts were, well this is the journey, the path and I need to sit and take some time to reflect and draw this part of the trip to a close. My instincts or whatever, tell me I need to do more and maybe I will, but for now let's rest a while and see what the sum of the parts are.

From the time when my dad died to now is 14 years, and where mum's concerned it's 12 years. The poetry started to flow after mum's death really and I've said about dad's death bringing me back to church. The road I've walked in all this time has been very odd and I thought that my understanding would improve as I became closer to God, but in reality, like the child growing up the next age bracket or milestone doesn't seem to bring any more understanding. The truth is I think, I have become closer and understanding is the wrong word, I am dealing with things differently and progressing my faith in a spiritual journey that quite often poses far more questions than it answers. The overriding and most important factor is though that I am speaking and praying in a way with more conviction and I feel my presence is being used constructively in His name. My life might be a wreck in my eyes but the acts the words, the things I do are being used to help bring His word to more of His children. My life in this world, on this earth, in a purely human fashion means very little in the scheme of nature and the millions on the earth, but it is what it is, performing and achieving as the greater body of Christ and even if I don't have the answers to questions like why did the recent Asian

Tsunami do what it did, why people still kill each other in Iraq and Palestine and Africa and AID's riddles the world. I can still bring peace and love and all the things that Jesus wanted us to do on His behalf. The reason for the pain and the suffering we can argue about forever, we can argue over the books we have with the words, but the real truth the real purpose of it all is in His hands and the way they guide us in our world. I was thinking about the temptations of life and the way we try to handle them, I also felt that we need as a Christian family to think carefully about what we are and what we feel. Human emotions are strange things and they can get easily confused, the human part of us is a strange chemistry set that is all too easily interfered with if not carefully looked after.

I think that the words of the next poem, a very recent one, is where I was reflecting upon my own weakness and mortal dilemma, judge for yourself if this is in anyway reminiscent of anything in your life, now in the past or likely to be in the future:

My Burden

My heart is heavy and my life lies heavy, Upon my shoulders I feel some great weight;

Only you can lift this from me, there is so much to tempt me, to make me veer away from a pathway laid for us.

My feelings, my life, the chemistry of my body such as it is here on this earth; I cannot have complete control and yet within my mind my soul I know what is and isn't right.

Why then is human flesh so weak, so inescapable some times, willing to do so much and yet so fragile, so easy to deflect.

So easy to have its own will, so easy to be blind, so easy to be deaf, so easy to be unloving.
So easy for the fragility of its short and sometimes difficult path -- to err and to bring upon it pain, and hurt, and upon its kindred ones, the same.

Why are some given the minds that anguish over what is done or not done, right or wrong, and yet some appear devoid of taking on this reasoning, this under-standing?

Or are they blind, or deaf and unfeeling not through lack of chemistry and mortal things, but because they know not, the rushing of the spirit, the cleans-ing, the essence that is Christ.

5ᵗʰ February 2005

You know we have strange affections, as I was sitting writing these last few bits for the book I gazed over the desk and there was a key ring with a model of a Vulcan bomber on it. This is a British built aircraft designed just after the Second World War, as we entered the so called "Cold War". It was designed to carry nuclear bombs over long distances if the occasion ever arose. The point I'm getting to is that this particular key ring was produced to help save the last of this aircraft's type. There appears to be a great deal of sentiment over this plane and many want to see it fly again. I have to admit that I do too, but why? It was a representation of the very worst of our nature, a weapon of war designed to carry payloads in the sky to kill people over long ranges using a bomb that produces the most awful results. Where oh where is the sense in that?

OK I know that we just want to see it's majesty as it flies through the air again, and in fairness it is a product of our abilities as humans and what we are capable of doing. Getting a number of tons of metalwork to fly at umpteen thousand feet above the earth is a great achievement and a gift that is bestowed upon us.

I used to work for Marconi Radar many years ago, until they decided to close the local branch and move to Chelmsford, I didn't go and so our paths parted. But during the twenty eight years I had with them I had the chance to see weapon systems being produced at first hand, I also had the chance to see them used too, as in 1982 our equipment was used in the war that the UK fought in the Falklands Islands. I was around 22 or so when I joined the company and to be honest I never really thought about the product in too much detail, I'd only recently married and was more interested in making a living. I saw many clever people at work though, electronic geniuses who made the systems work and discovered the mistakes when the kit malfunctioned or just didn't work. These were the times when something got overlooked or not enough money was available to make something so corners needed to be cut or some "pruning" took place because the budget was being overspent.

The fact is that the warship we made radar for, had serious problems due to the budget constraints placed upon it, not only the ship itself but the systems used. You see we can only make what is affordable, (or to the technology that is available to us) and various Governments always think that they can do more with the money they have and then discover they can't. The problem is that when the ships with all the wonderful kit we built were tested, they soon found the weaknesses and as a result people died. It was very difficult for us too as we thought that what we had made was the best, but it was not because we had been forced to build to a budget.

How often do we go around museums? Especially war museums looking at the battles and the equipment used? How we marvel at the innovations used and how we shudder at the slaughter, especially the first world war, and also the barbaric way that we killed each other using swords and battle axes and so on. All made to a budget, all designed by a human being for the purpose they have.

So where is this leading to? I said that I thought how we have strange affections when I looked at the "cold war bomber", and we do. The affections we have for the natural things, flowers, clouds on high, rain falling down on the earth, sunlight that warms us and keeps us alive, little animals that live around us and with us. Were these built to a budget? And why do we have this insatiable desire to see things that we made years before as war material or even the reminders of our past. It is all the way that we live our lives and contact each other and use the gifts that God gave us, and marvel at the wonderful world that he has given us to have and to use and to use our gifts our talents, and of course our strange affections.

The Light of the World?

Into the eyes streams the light of the world
The universe, stars, the greatness unfurled.
Seeking the reasons for the sights that you see,
Can you explain them, give reasons, why can you see?

Look to the heavens the planets, the stars all there in line;
What does it mean, could this be a sign?
Laughing and smiling see the face of the child,
The parents the family, loving these moments so tender so mild.

Just touch the mother the father the daughter the son;
Triumphing always, seeing goodness and love we've almost won.
Stare for a moment at the dawn of each day,
Feel the warmth, see the sunlight the colours that stray.

Marvel at the wonder of storm clouds on high
Raindrops there falling and the earth breathes a sigh.
What have your eyes seen here, can you tell me true?
Look deep again, embrace the vast view.

The images seen by your eyes, do they tell it true?
But when is the payback, just when is it due?
Never, no never, do you need to claim?
Who was the author, the builder, the one with the aim?

Truly the vision the point of your eyes,
Is to see all of these wonders and what really applies.
Your eyes are the way that you view this great place
But the real light is not seen by the eyes in your face.

The soul takes the light that is intended for you,
Use the soul as the eyes that's all that you do,
Remember that eyes are used for the sight;
But it's your soul that is used to accept the real might.

30th October 2002 (At work)

137

Final chapters sometimes make me think of a summing up of what preceded and to an extent I'd sort of thought of doing just that. But then you've already read the book to this point so why do I need to recoup?. It's probably because not being a "writer" as such I need or needed, to think about what's been said why I said it and what's this final chapter anyway.

The truth is that this is the end of this book and I've struggled to end it really as more things happen to me and more things occur which I feel should be going into the pages of this.

I can't do that otherwise the book will never finish as I've been fiddling around with this for about three or four years I need to draw a line and say this one finishes here. I have already some thoughts for the next journey into another book, who knows? Besides what is the book about and what has it expressed? I think that its been a journey of some twelve years or so and where that journey has taken me. There's an awful lot of omissions in the journey and the book as it stands and maybe a reprise of the twelve years and maybe even further, is needed. But no matter, I've said what I wanted to say so far; the future, well that's happening all the time and who knows what's there for any of us?

I tried looking back on my life whilst putting this book together, which has been fairly haphazard at best, bit like my life in some respects. I have had many tragedies in my life, personal events that have been difficult to understand and even more difficult to live with. Have you ever done a misdeed or something so evil that you whole being shudders when you try to recall it? Maybe you haven't, maybe you never will, maybe it's just around the corner, even so what do we with these? Carry them around with us like all the other baggage of life we accumulate over the short span of time we're here? And what do they do for us? What do they make us? Only we who carry these burdens can know.

In my life I have been very lucky really, I've never known the hardships of the AID's victims, or the Tsunami disaster, no all my hardships have been the usual day to day disasters we all have to handle, the deaths of dear ones, financial crises, handling life that is thrown at us in our little lives. But who is to say that these are any less important in the grand scheme of things?

The Christian path, any path for that matter that we tread is going to have events in it, so how are they going to be handled? You may take the view that you are capable of fighting your own battles and don't need a "Christ" or "God" to support you, there are lots of good friends and people around you that can help, or if you are that way inclined, that you can step upon or climb over to maintain your position in life or the particular way you're going.

I suppose the choice of how we live out our lives is very much ours, the free will we have allows that. It won't make the slightest bit of difference in the scheme of things if I'm rude to some one in the street or don't do something that offends that other person, unless you're on the receiving end! Then how do you respond and what do you think of that person, me in particular. Does this matter? Certainly not to me especially if I don't care about it.

Then the discontent, the opportunity, of social regression, civil unrest, war who knows but these are the very seeds of that discontent and evil. We sow and so shall we reap, but you will decide and you will also decide who in the final chapter decides on what we did or didn't do.

So here we are, I ask the question again, what of us? What does God, your God, his God anybodies God, make of us? Because I'm born a white English speaking man does that diminish my worth, just as much as a black Somali speaking woman, does that legacy mean anything?, so why was Jesus Christ a Jew?. The amount of people out there who'd immediately jump up and explain why and what the reasons are for this based on their assumptions and understanding of the Bible the Koran and any Holy Book you wish to put forward –
but what do they actually provide us with? Ask the mother of a dying child in Africa to judge the arguments, ask the defiled the raped the murdered, the slain from suicide bombs, the mountains of bodies in Auschwitz ask them all, they wouldn't give you a single lead or answer to all your fancy thoughts or words, they would just want the Love of God, pure and simple, nothing to do with how the Koran was written or by whom, or by when or whom the Bible was either. No all the scholars from time immemorial don't add up to any worth other than we all crave Gods love and we all need that and the fact is that religion overall stifles the true meaning that God had and has for us all.

Argue all you like about the texts and how we should be and what we should be but in plain terms mankind hasn't a clue without God. We make rules and regulations without a thought of why they'll be broken and judge on the basis of our belief, but in the final additions when all is come to an end and we draw our last breath, only then will anyone know who was right and did we do right.

I do believe that this journey is at the point where it needs to rest and I need to put the last words together, I feel that a poem to end with would be right and through the poems the words that are written for all I wish God's presence in your life and always.

In the Skies

I see you through the blue and grey skies, all the wonders that are you:
I can see the wonder of all who love me, who love you, who love the world
we are:
And I and you and all know joy and unhappiness and illness and many
things of strife.

And yet these are as nothing when through those eyes that see the reality of
it all is totally revealed.
Take the notes that make the scales, the music of our world, and take the
alphabets the letters of all the tongues upon this earth;

For without the rhythms the compositions or the languages, the written
words, what are they but jumbled pieces meaningless signs, nothing.
But placed together, harmoniously and as they should be done -- we have
the revelation, the wonder of what they are all for.

8th March 2005

Printed in the United Kingdom
by Lightning Source UK Ltd.
122998UK00001B/259-330/A